HIGH-ALTITUDE
BREAKFAST

SWEET & SAVORY BAKING AT 5,000 FEET & ABOVE

NICOLE HAMPTON

OF THE BLOG

WEST
MARGIN
PRESS

For Jacob:
Your toast,
my eggs

CONTENTS

EASY LIKE SUNDAY MORNING

Hi there! I'm Nicole, and I've been baking in a high-altitude kitchen for most of my life. It doesn't have to baffle you, and you can still make the recipes that you've always loved at sea-level. This book is centered around my love for breakfast foods and my love for making things from scratch, even in my challenging, high-elevation climate.

I want to be able to make my own English muffins, and then turn them into amazing sandwiches. I love to make cheese-filled bread, and then turn it into cheese toast, and even savory French toast. That's what we're doing here—taking our breakfast baking to the next level with from-scratch recipes that will make for the most special brunches and morning meals!

I'm a proponent of enjoying breakfast at any time of day, and if that's not one of the biggest perks of adulthood, I don't know what is. We eat breakfast food so much in my house that it was literally a part of my husband's wedding vows! When I was a kid, and my dad was out for the evening, my mom and I would treat ourselves to breakfast for dinner—it's one of my favorite memories. My dad made us fried eggs and rice almost every Saturday morning, and I still don't think I can fry an egg just like him.

High-altitude baking can feel like a confusing thing, and I think for many people it makes them believe they aren't good bakers. I spent years of my life trying to figure out why my cakes were sinking; why my bread was dense; and why nothing seemed to turn out of my oven the way it should. When I first started baking from scratch in my Denver-area home, there were so few resources available about high-altitude baking that it was a major trial and error adventure.

Baking brings me such genuine joy, and it's one of my favorite parts of life. I often hear from people who lived at sea-level and moved to a high-altitude area, only to find that their once-loved recipes no longer work. My ultimate goal is to bring the ability to bake back to everyone living in a higher elevation, and to share the delight that baking brings me every day. If there's one thing I've learned over the past 10 years of baking, it's that everyone uses different methods for adapting high-altitude recipes. After developing hundreds of recipes over the years, I'm sharing what I know to work best. But if you have a secret method for making your cakes rise at altitude, keep at it. If it works, it works!

In addition to the more than 80 irresistible recipes that I developed and tested in my 5,000-feet-above-sea-level kitchen, this book has dozens of tips and tricks to adapt your own recipes for high-altitude baking. I wrote this book because, for me, there's nothing more special than making a big Saturday morning family breakfast. Or making pancakes on a Tuesday night when it just seems like the right choice. Breakfast baking is an important part of life for me, and everyone, no matter where they live, should be able to enjoy it. I hope these recipes make it into your kitchen too!

TOOLS & INGREDIENTS

Every successful baker will tell you, whether they live at sea level or on top of a mountain or anywhere in between, that an important secret to success is having the right tools and ingredients on hand for every baking task. In this section I talk about the must-have tools and equipment that you need to bake a variety of different types of baked goods. I also reveal some other items that are nice to have (i.e., I find them helpful, but you can still bake my recipes if you don't have them). Next, I list out a number of ingredients that are I use for my high-altitude baking and why they're important.

ESSENTIAL TOOLS

When it comes to baking, half the battle is having the tools you need, when you need them.

Here's what I consider the necessary items to make the recipes in this book, and for most baking in general:

- Mixing bowls both large and small, at least some of them microwave- and heat-safe. A good glass nesting set is a great place to start, and you can find them inexpensively online.
- Measuring spoons and cups in both dry measure and wet measure forms. I use glass measuring cups for everything from measuring liquids to microwave-melting butter, and for stirring together small quantities of ingredients. If you're a really serious baker, you may consider getting multiple sets of dry measuring cups and spoons and several glass liquid measuring cups to make sure you've always got what you need.

- Whisks are essential to beat your ingredients and for a great many hand-mixed recipes. When it comes to hand tools, whisks are top of the list for me.
- Wooden spoons are useful to help mix doughs by hand when you're not using a mixer.
- Rubber spatulas are my go-to items to scrape and stir things together. I prefer silicone spatulas that are all one piece of the same material, which helps prevent moisture from getting inside of them.
- Pancake flipper/egg flipper spatulas are for, you guessed it, flipping pancakes, eggs, and the like. If you are a fan of big pancakes, nothing can beat a large sturdy pancake flipper!
- A pastry blender makes quick work of cutting butter into dry ingredients, which makes preparing biscuits and scones easy.
- Cake pans and bakeware in all shapes and sizes are a must. I always prefer metal baking pans, and in fact almost never use glass. You'll need a 12-cup muffin tin, 8-inch square and round cake pans, a loaf pan, and Bundt pans. Additionally, a good sturdy rimmed baking sheet pan is vital.
- Parchment paper is a kitchen workhorse, but you can use nonstick baking sheets if you prefer. I use parchment paper in cake pans and loaf pans regularly to help easily remove whatever I've baked up.
- A box grater with both wide and thin grating sides comes in very handy in the baker's kitchen. A microplane is super helpful for zesting citrus.
- An electric hand mixer helps get batters and doughs well mixed. There are a good deal of recipes that can be hand-mixed, but

even more that will come together much better, and much faster, with the help of an electric mixer.

- An instant-read thermometer helps you take the temperatures of milk for blooming yeast, bread once baked, and everything in between. Often in baking, things need to be precise, and this tool makes all the difference. If you like to fry things, such as doughnuts, a deep-frying thermometer is also important.
- Skillets for cooking pancakes, French toast, eggs, and fillings are a must. A 10-inch skillet is a great place to start.

NICE-TO-HAVE TOOLS

The following tools are optional, but if you are a regular baker, you'll be glad you have them on hand.

- Food processors, both large and small, will save you lots of time. It may seem excessive to have two of these tools, but a large processor is great for grating up a big batch of carrots or cheese, or for making a whole crust for a quiche. But a small processor is more of a daily tool, and I use mine to finely chop nuts, blend up dried fruits, and crush up crackers.
- A stand mixer can help you multitask in the kitchen. Especially useful for kneading bread and pizza doughs, it can do all the hard work for you along the way.
- Biscuit cutters, or cookie cutters that are about the size of biscuits, are very helpful. You can use a mason jar lid, or you can make square biscuits by cutting with a knife, but cutters are easiest!
- Very sharp knives for all the slicing and dicing are a godsend. I love to have three main knives in my drawer at all times: a 5- to 6-inch utility knife, a very sharp serrated knife, and a cleaver. I know the cleaver doesn't seem like the most practical

knife, but I actually find it to be what I am most comfortable with when chopping up large items, or large quantities.

- A rolling pin, of course, helps roll out doughs. You can, however, absolutely use a wine bottle if you don't have a pin!
- Cooling racks are helpful for cooling everything, but also to set inside of a rimmed baking sheet and into a low oven to keep pancakes and waffles warm as you continue cooking.

HIGH-ALTITUDE BAKING INGREDIENTS

I'm not going to be the person who tells you to splurge on the $12 carton of eggs, or the pound of expensive European butter. As a home baker, I pretty much always find myself on a budget, and I can tell you with absolute confidence that you can make exceptional baked goods with store-brand ingredients. If you feel like you want to splurge on a fancy cheese, or the good eggs, absolutely go for it and you'll have something wonderful. But if not, your baked goods are still going to be delicious!

I do have some guidelines you should consider when it comes to ingredients for this book, and this is standby advice that applies to all my recipes and most baking recipes in general.

- Butter should always be unsalted for baking, and every recipe in this book that calls for butter has been developed with unsalted butter.
- Eggs are always large in my house. They are the most readily available in most grocery stores, and they work perfectly in most recipes.
- Vanilla extract is an expensive ingredient, so get what you can. I am known to hunt for sales on vanilla, and to hoard it whenever possible. I also have a jar of

homemade vanilla extract, which is just vanilla beans and vodka, and you can keep feeding it with more vanilla beans and vodka basically forever. It's great to have on hand, and you can give vanilla bean pods a second life after scraping the seeds out for a recipe!

- Flour can be a bit tricky. I try to call for all-purpose whenever possible, but if a recipe calls for bread flour, cake flour, or even pastry flour, it's extremely important to use the right flour in order for a recipe to work.

- Sugars are usually pretty straightforward. This book has recipes that use granulated sugar, powdered sugar, and brown sugar. I always use dark brown sugar for a deep flavor.

- Cocoa powder is something that I use often in baking, and I always use Dutch process cocoa powder. It provides a deep chocolate flavor, and over the years I have found that extremely beneficial in baking anything chocolatey. It's commonly available in grocery stores near me, and often labeled as "Dark Cocoa Powder." I find that it can almost always be swapped out in a recipe in place of natural cocoa.

- Dried herbs are something that I use frequently as a home baker, but they can easily be swapped out for fresh herbs and ingredients if preferred. You'll want to use about twice as much of the fresh herbs versus the dried.

- Yeast in my recipes always refers to active dry yeast, which is easiest to find in most grocery stores today. You can use rapid-rise yeast in a pinch, but it will, as you may have guessed, make your dough rise faster, so you'll need to keep a close eye on it to avoid overproofing.

HIGH-ALTITUDE BAKING PRIMER

If you used to live at sea-level, or if you're just starting out baking for the first time at high-altitude, you probably already know the struggles. One of the most important things that I like to share with people is how to fix recipes to match their current elevation. I know how discouraging it can be to spend the time baking something only to have it turn out terribly, and we don't need that in our lives!

I still feel like I learn and become a better baker every day, even after years spent and hundreds of recipes developed, but once you know how to adjust recipes, everything becomes a little easier. If you're baking for the first time at altitude, here are some of the most common results that you might see:

- Cakes that sink in the middle during or after baking
- Super dense yeast breads that lack flavor
- Batters that take way longer than the suggested time to bake through
- Cookies that spread too much and become super thin
- Baked goods that turn out bland even though you haven't forgotten any ingredients

Now that I know the right adjustments to make, I almost never run into these issues anymore–even on my first try adapting a sea-level recipe. Follow my tips below and you'll be baking up a storm in no time!

HOW TO ADJUST RECIPES FOR HIGH-ALTITUDE BAKING

There's no one-step fix-all that you can make to your baking recipes for perfect results every time. Instead, I like to approach recipes in groups. For example, you won't make the same adjustments to muffins that you make to yeasted bread. But if you know how to handle each type of recipe, you can adjust anything to work at the altitude where you live now.

Cakes Let's take it from the top, which is almost always cakes. I find that cakes are the most common recipes that bakers want to tackle, and it makes perfect sense. Bringing a decadent coffee cake to a special-occasion brunch is the ultimate gift. I have also always considered cakes to be the hardest type of baked good to adjust for altitude. There's a lot that can go wrong, but it's fixable. Here's how I approach a sea-level recipe for cake:

- Decrease the amount of leavening agents by 25 percent. For example, if a recipe calls for 1 teaspoon of baking powder, reduce it to ¾ teaspoon. At altitude, baked goods tend to rise faster while baking, and then collapse before they are cooked through, causing sinking in the middle.
- Add more flour, which helps to give cake more structure as it bakes. I typically add ¼ to ½ cup more flour to my dry ingredients, depending on how much cake a recipe makes. For example, if you're making a large Bundt cake you'll have a lot of cake batter, so go for more flour!
- Reduce the sugar just slightly. The faster that liquid evaporates (and it will evaporate more quickly at altitude), the more concentrated the sugar will be, which can cause issues with the structure of your cakes. As a general rule, I like to reduce sugar by 1 tablespoon per cup of sugar called for in the recipe.

- Increase the liquid in a recipe slightly. Whether that's milk or water, I like to increase it by 1 to 2 tablespoons in most cases. Liquid evaporates faster in higher altitudes, which can greatly affect the texture of a cake and also how flavorful it is.
- Bake the cake for longer than a recipe calls for. It can take longer to bake recipes at altitude, so you want to keep a closer eye on the visual cues in a recipe. Once the cake looks set in the middle and no longer jiggles, start testing it with a toothpick inserted into the center. If the toothpick comes out clean, your cake is finished!
- Grease your cake pans very well! This may not only apply to high altitude, but rumor has it here that cakes stick more in high altitude. I grease all my cake pans with this mix: equal parts shortening, canola oil, and flour. Beat the ingredients together until completely smooth, and store in the fridge to have on hand for future use.

Yeasted Breads I struggled with bread making for years, and I think it was due in part to my altitude, and in part to normal struggles and the learning curve of making really good bread. In either case, practice makes perfect, and I've got some really helpful tips for you:

- Keep a close watch as your dough rises. Bread dough often rises faster at high altitude than at sea level, so you may see your dough puff up long before a sea-level recipe says it will. I like to snap a quick picture of the dough on my smartphone for reference and just keep an eye on it so it doesn't overproof. An overproofed dough will either not rise while baking, or it could rise and then collapse because the increased gas in the dough compromises its structure.

- Decrease your goal size for the dough's rise. When a recipe calls for the dough to double in size, move on to the next recipe step just before the doubled stage. This also helps prevent overproofing.
- Knead the dough longer than you think you need to. Once I realized I wasn't kneading my dough long enough, the quality of all my bread improved dramatically. I almost always knead for a full 10 to 15 minutes. In most cases your dough should be very elastic and very smooth. The dough will also absorb more of the flour as you knead, and you may find you need less flour to reach this stage than you thought, so be sure to add your flour slowly, and give it time to knead into the dough.
- Use an instant-read thermometer when baking your bread. Since it can take longer to bake at altitude, it can be hard to know when bread dough is baked through. For a typical loaf-style bread, the internal temperature should reach 185°F to 190°F.

Quick Breads, Scones, and Muffins
Quick breads are a category of baking that use a chemical leavener (baking powder or baking soda) instead of yeast. They include coffee cakes and some loaf breads as well as biscuits, scones, muffins, and other items that aren't super sweet. These recipes are usually fairly simple to make, but you should still keep some things in mind for adaptations:

- Avoid overmixing a batter or overworking a dough. You'll often see cues to mix until "just incorporated," which means you don't need a batter to be smooth and lump-free, but you just want to mix it until there are no dry pockets of flour remaining.
- It's important to reach a golden-brown top for these types of baked goods. If the item

does not achieve a golden-brown color at the suggested bake time, raise the oven temperature by 25 degrees and reduce the baking time the next time you bake the recipe.

- Particularly with muffins, moisture can be an issue at altitude. Consider adding an additional 2 to 3 teaspoons of water or whatever liquid you are using in the batter. Another option is to add ¼ cup of sour cream to a muffin recipe that yields 12 muffins.
- For muffins and batter-based recipes, add 2 to 4 tablespoons of flour to the dry ingredients to increase the overall structure.
- For batter-based recipes, reduce the leavening by 25 percent to slow the rising process while your dish bakes.
- Let your batters and doughs rest before baking. For scones and biscuits, this often comes in the form of a cold rest, which helps the butter chill back down so it can properly puff and flake in the oven. For muffins, a rest period helps to activate the baking powder and baking soda, which results in a taller domed top after baking.

Pancakes and Waffles Pancakes and waffles are similar to quick breads when it comes to the adjustments needed, even though they don't cook in the oven. Without adjustments for the altitude, you may find that your pancakes and waffles end up a bit flat, without much rise, and lacking in flavor.

- Avoid overmixing your batter. It may seem odd, but it's actually good to have lumps in the batter running throughout, and I always opt to mix the batter by hand.
- I recommend adding 2 to 4 tablespoons of flour to your dry ingredients—this will help give your batter a good structure.

- Reduce the leavening in a sea-level recipe by 25 percent to slow the rising process. This helps make sure that the batter doesn't rise too much while cooking, causing a collapse that results in flat pancakes and waffles.
- Be sure to let your batter rest before cooking. This allows the baking powder and baking soda to react with the other ingredients in the batter gently and slowly, making for a bigger rise and a fluffier end result.

Cookies As I mentioned before, cookies are generally the least affected item when it comes to high-altitude adaptations. However, there are still some good points to remember if you're working with a cookie that isn't turning out quite right (and who doesn't like a good cookie plate at the end of a weekend brunch?):

- It can be tough to find the right baking time for cookies. Most recipes give a range for bake times, mainly because you have to keep an eye on the cookies in those last few minutes to avoid under- or overbaking. I suggest doing a test batch with one or two cookies at first, which will help you figure out the right baking time in your particular oven.
- Beat the butter and sugar together really well. For years I didn't fully understand the importance of this. I suggest at least 2 to 3 full minutes of beating before continuing with the recipe.
- Some people worry about overmixing cookie dough and, of course, it's important to avoid doing so, but it's also important not to undermix. At the last stage of mixing, when the last set of ingredients goes into the batter, make sure you get everything completely and evenly incorporated, even if it seems like you are

mixing for a long time. Otherwise, you'll end up with an uneven batch of cookies that don't bake at the same rate and are inconsistent.

- Reduce the leavening in cookies the same way you do for cakes, by 25 percent. This will help prevent cookies from becoming too puffy and spreading too much.
- If your cookie recipe is spreading super thin when you bake it, add an additional 2 to 4 tablespoons of flour to the recipe to provide more structure.

Savory Cooking Savory cooking and things that you make on the stovetop are generally less affected by the altitude, but you'll still find that some small adjustments make a big difference:

- Add more liquid to stovetop-based dishes. Similar to baking foods in the oven, liquids will evaporate more quickly at higher altitudes. For example, when cooking rice, you may find that your liquid has been absorbed into the rice, but the rice isn't quite done. To combat this, add another couple tablespoons of liquid to balance the effect and cook the rice for a few minutes longer. Oatmeal can have similar issues, and I recommend the same adjustments here.
- Boiled eggs and poached eggs can take a little longer to cook. It's usually just a couple of minutes longer, but you won't see quite the same results as sea-level for cooking eggs.

OTHER HIGH-ALTITUDE BAKING NOTES

With these tips, I'm confident you'll be able to make your sea-level recipes work for you at altitude. It's such a good feeling to be able to successfully bake a Bundt cake for a friend, or to make a cozy from-scratch breakfast for your family, and you can totally do it!

These tricks have changed the way I bake and the results that I see every single day. However, it's important to remember that different altitudes present different issues. I bake at about 5,000 feet above sea level, and I find that most people who live between 3,000 feet and 7,500 feet or so above sea level do not need to make any adjustments to my recipes. However, if you're up higher than that, you may find you need to take my tips from above and push them a little further—add a touch more flour, a touch less baking powder, and so on. These adjustments will still serve you, but the higher you are, the more you may find you need to tweak recipes to make them perfect!

Living at higher altitudes is wonderful for so many reasons, but baking isn't always one of them. Figuring out ways to adjust recipes and working through some basic recipes that I can twist into something new has brought me back to baking time and time again, even though I've had more failures in the kitchen than I'd like to admit.

I hope that, through this book, you will find new ways to bake incredibly yummy baked goods for breakfast—or anytime. Cheers to filling our stomachs with good food as much as we possibly can!

BREADS

Yeasted breads and quick breads are something that you find in so many breakfast dishes today, and who doesn't want to start out the day with a few carbs? Quick bread is the real path to the world of cake for breakfast, so don't be afraid to whip up a loaf of rich pumpkin bread to go with your coffee! Whether you want to make your own English muffins, bagels, or a cheesy, savory, twisty bread to serve with breakfast, learning how to make bread is one of the most rewarding ways to start baking.

BASIC WHITE BREAD

This is a super simple recipe for a fluffy white loaf of bread. It's perfect for sandwiches and toast, and I use it all the time because it's so easy and flavorful. If you're a beginner bread-baker, this is a great place to start. Use this bread for: Caramelized Onion & Egg Toast (page 149), Stuffed French Toast (page 162), Savory French Toast with Hollandaise (page 166), Blueberry French Toast Bake (page 161), Breakfast Grilled Cheese (page 187), and Breakfast Panzanella (page 196).

In a microwave-safe bowl, combine the milk, water, honey, sugar, and 1 tablespoon butter. Heat in the microwave on high power in 30-second increments until it reads 110°F to 115°F on an instant-read thermometer. Stir in the yeast, and set aside to bloom until the mixture is bubbly and foamy, about 5 minutes.

Transfer the yeast mixture to the bowl of a stand mixer fitted with a paddle attachment (or into a large mixing bowl) and add 2 cups of flour along with the salt. Mix until combined with the mixer on low speed or with a wooden spoon. The mixture will be liquidy and lumpy at this point.

Add in another cup of flour and continue to mix, adding more flour in ¼-cup portions until the dough starts to pull away from the sides of the bowl. If using a stand mixer, switch to a dough hook attachment at this point. The dough should be soft and slightly sticky when you stop adding flour. Knead either in the mixer or by hand until the dough is elastic. By mixer, this will take about 5 minutes, and by hand it should take about 10 minutes. The dough may still be slightly lumpy but should spring back when you touch it.

MAKES 1 LOAF

1 cup whole milk

¾ cup water

2 tablespoons honey

2 tablespoons sugar

1 tablespoon butter

2½ teaspoons active dry yeast

4 to 5 cups all-purpose flour

2½ teaspoons salt

Cooking spray

3 tablespoons butter, melted

CONTINUED ON NEXT PAGE

Transfer the dough to a lightly oiled large bowl and cover with plastic wrap. Let the dough rise in a warm, draft-free spot by about one-third its size, which takes about 30 minutes for me; keep an eye on your dough size to avoid overproofing.

With cooking spray, grease an 8- or 9-inch loaf pan and set aside. Lightly flour your work surface. Using a rolling pin, roll out your dough into a large rectangle. The long side should be about the same length as the length of your loaf pan. Starting on the loaf-pan-length side, use your hands to roll the dough into a tight log and place it seam-side down in the prepared loaf pan. Cover with plastic wrap and let the dough rest for about 15 minutes. Meanwhile, preheat your oven to 375°F. The dough will be just slightly puffed when ready to bake.

Brush the top of the loaf generously with some of the melted butter and bake until deep golden brown, 45 to 48 minutes. If you like, you can use an instant-read thermometer to check for doneness; the inside should reach 195°F.

Brush the remaining melted butter over the top of the loaf immediately when you take it out of the oven. Cool for about 20 minutes in the pan, then turn out onto a rack to finish cooling. Wait until the bread is completely cool to slice. Enjoy!

BRIOCHE

Brioche is a rich, buttery loaf that is delicious on its own, but just screams to be made into French toast (see the French Toast Dippers on page 165). It takes a bit more work to make than your standard bread—and it's the perfect project to pull out your stand mixer for—but it's so worth it! I'm using a cooked flour paste in this recipe, called a tangzhong, and it helps create the soft, pillowy bread that you've always dreamed of.

To make the flour paste, in a small saucepan, whisk together the milk and flour, heating over medium-high heat or until it becomes a very thick paste, 2 to 3 minutes. Set aside to cool.

To make the bread, heat the milk in the microwave on high heat in 30-second increments until it reads about 115°F on an instant-read thermometer. In a large bowl, or in the bowl of a stand mixer fitted with the dough hook attachment, mix together the warmed milk, sugar, and yeast, and let stand for 5 minutes.

Add 2 of the whole eggs and the egg yolk and mix to combine with the mixer on low speed or with a wooden spoon. Add 2 cups flour, the cooked flour paste, and salt. Mix together until the dough becomes smooth, and all flour is incorporated, adding more if needed. The dough should be tacky and sticking to the bottom of the bowl but should pull away clean.

At this stage, the dough will still be rather sticky to the touch. Add in the butter 1 tablespoon at a time and continue to knead until the butter is incorporated. If you are working without a mixer, knead in the dough by hand. It will be a bit messy at first, but will eventually come together.

MAKES 1 LOAF

FOR THE FLOUR PASTE:
¼ cup whole milk
2 tablespoons flour

FOR THE BRIOCHE:
½ cup whole milk
3 tablespoons sugar
2¼ teaspoons active dry yeast
3 eggs
1 egg yolk
2½ to 3 cups all-purpose flour
1 teaspoon salt
¼ cup butter, softened
Cooking spray

CONTINUED ON NEXT PAGE

Continue kneading until the dough is smooth and pulls away from the sides of the bowl, about 10 minutes in a mixer or 20 minutes by hand. Place in a large, clean, buttered bowl, and cover with plastic wrap or a clean dishtowel. Let the dough rise in a warm, draft-free spot until it is nearly double in size. For me, this takes about 30 to 40 minutes. However, you should really keep an eye on your dough rather than the time!

After the first rise, knead the dough once or twice with your hands, return it to the bowl, and cover. Place in the refrigerator until the dough rises by about one-third its size. Again, keep an eye on your dough for this. For me, this takes about 1 hour; keep in mind that chilling the dough slows the rising process.

Remove the dough from the refrigerator and let it rest at room temperature for 20 minutes. Using cooking spray, lightly grease an 8-inch loaf pan and set aside. Lightly flour your work surface. Using a rolling pin, roll out your dough into a large rectangle. The long side should be about the same length as the length of your loaf pan. Starting on the loaf-pan-length side, use your hands to roll the dough into a tight log and place it seam-side down into the prepared loaf pan. Cover with plastic wrap and let the dough rest for about 20 minutes. Meanwhile, preheat your oven to 400°F. You'll only see a slight change in the size of the dough when it's ready to bake.

In a small bowl, beat the remaining egg until blended and brush the top of the loaf generously with the beaten egg. Bake the loaf until the top has become golden and shiny from the egg wash, 35 to 40 minutes. Let cool completely, then slice and enjoy!

PUMPKIN BREAD

This isn't your classic pumpkin loaf, but instead a yeasted loaf of bread with all the flavors of pumpkin that you love. You can make it sweet by adding warm spices, or savory by adding dried sage, rosemary, and black pepper. It will become a new favorite breakfast bread, but you can also use it in Pumpkin French Toast (page 154).

In a microwave-safe bowl, stir together the milk, melted butter, and sugar. Heat the mixture in the microwave on high power in 30-second increments until the mixture reaches 110°F on an instant-read thermometer, and then stir in the yeast. Let the mixture stand until it's foamy and bubbly, about 5 minutes.

In the bowl of a stand mixer fitted with the dough hook attachment or in a large bowl, stir together the pumpkin puree, 2 of the eggs, and the bloomed yeast mixture. Add in 4 cups of flour, the salt, and your spice mixture of choice for either a sweet or savory loaf.

Mix on medium speed until the dough becomes very elastic, adding more flour if needed. The dough should be soft and slightly tacky, but should not stick to your hands. In a stand mixer, it should ball up around the dough hook and pull away from the bowl. In a stand mixer, this should take about 10 minutes of kneading, and it should take 15 to 20 minutes of kneading by hand. Leave the dough in your bowl and cover it with plastic wrap. Let the dough rise in a warm, draft-free spot by about one-third its size. For me, this takes 20 to 30 minutes. Be sure to watch your dough carefully, as it could be different in your kitchen.

MAKES 1 LOAF

⅓ cup milk

¼ cup butter, melted

2 tablespoons sugar

2¼ teaspoons active dry yeast

1¼ cups prepared pumpkin puree

3 eggs

4 to 5 cups all-purpose flour

2 teaspoons salt

FOR A SWEET LOAF:

1½ teaspoons ground cinnamon

¾ teaspoon ground ginger

½ teaspoon ground nutmeg

¼ teaspoon ground cloves

¼ teaspoon ground allspice

FOR A SAVORY LOAF:

½ teaspoon salt

2 teaspoons dried sage

1 teaspoon dried rosemary

½ teaspoon freshly ground black pepper

Cooking spray

CONTINUED ON NEXT PAGE

PUMPKIN BREAD (CONTINUED)

Lightly spray an 8-inch loaf pan with cooking spray and set aside. Using a rolling pin, roll out your dough into a large rectangle on a lightly floured surface. The long side should be about the same length as the length of your loaf pan. Starting on the loaf-pan-length side, use your hands to roll the dough into a tight log and place it seam-side down into the prepared loaf pan. Cover with plastic wrap or a clean dishtowel and let the dough rest for about 20 minutes. Meanwhile, preheat your oven to 375°F.

In a small bowl, beat the remaining egg, and brush the top of the dough generously with it. Bake until the top is a deep golden brown, and the internal temperature reaches about 190°F on an instant-read thermometer, 40 to 45 minutes. Let cool completely in the pan before removing, slicing, and serving!

CHOCOLATE CHUNK CRANBERRY BREAD

I'm using the same tangzhong method that I use in my Brioche (page 23), and the fluffiness it brings to the bread helps prevent the filled bread from getting too dense. This one is studded with dark chocolate chunks and dried cranberries for a tart bite that is a wonderful treat on its own, let alone as French toast! Use it for Banana-Chocolate Toast (page 150) or Chocolate-Cranberry French Toast (page 157).

To make the flour paste, in a small saucepan, cook the ¼ cup milk and the flour over medium heat, whisking constantly, until it forms a very thick paste. Set aside to cool.

To make the bread, in a microwave-safe bowl, stir together 1 cup of the milk, sugar, and vanilla extract. Heat in the microwave on high power in 30-second increments until it reaches 115°F on an instant-read thermometer. Pour the mixture into the bowl of a stand mixer fitted with the dough hook attachment or into a large bowl and stir in the yeast. Let the mixture stand until it becomes foamy and bubbly, about 5 minutes.

Stir in the egg and oil, and then add in 2½ cups of the flour, the cocoa powder, and salt. Knead the dough together using the dough hook on medium speed or by hand for 10 to 15 minutes. The dough should be very elastic, and will stick to the bottom of the bowl slightly, but will pull away from the sides of the bowl. Cover the bowl with plastic wrap, and let the dough rise in a warm, draft-free spot until it has almost doubled in size, which takes about 30 to 45 minutes for me.

MAKES 1 LOAF

FOR THE FLOUR PASTE:

¼ cup whole milk

¼ cup all-purpose flour

FOR THE BREAD:

1 cup plus 1 tablespoon whole milk

3 tablespoons sugar

1 teaspoon vanilla extract

2¼ teaspoons active dry yeast

1 egg

¼ cup vegetable oil

2½ to 3 cups all-purpose flour, plus more for rolling

¼ cup Dutch process cocoa powder

1 teaspoon salt

3½ ounces dark chocolate, chopped into small pieces

⅓ cup dried cranberries, roughly chopped

Cooking spray

CONTINUED ON NEXT PAGE

CHOCOLATE CHUNK CRANBERRY BREAD
(CONTINUED)

Lightly grease an 8-inch loaf pan with cooking spray and set aside. Place the dough on a lightly floured work surface. Using a rolling pin, roll out your dough into a large rectangle. The shorter side should be about the length of your loaf pan. Sprinkle the chopped dark chocolate and the chopped cranberries evenly across the dough. Then, starting on the short side, use your hands to roll up the dough into a tight log. Place the log seam-side down in your prepared pan and cover with plastic wrap. Let the dough rise in a warm, draft-free spot for about 20 minutes. Preheat your oven to 375°F. The dough will puff just slightly during this short rise.

Brush the top of your loaf with the remaining 1 tablespoon milk. Bake until the internal temperature of the bread registers about 190°F when tested with an instant-read thermometer and it sounds hollow when tapped on the bottom, 40 to 45 minutes.

Cool the bread for 15 minutes in the pan, and then turn it out onto a wire rack to finish cooling. Slice and enjoy!

CINNAMON SWIRL BREAD

This is a versatile, fluffy white bread with a cinnamon swirl running through it. Warning: It's going to make your house smell amazing, and it makes the most amazing toast! My mom always loves a good cinnamon swirl toast, and so do I. If you want something more than toast, try it in Strawberry Toast (page 146) and Cinnamon Bread Pudding (page 204).

In a microwave-safe bowl, stir together the milk, water, honey, sugar, butter, and vanilla extract. Heat the mixture in the microwave on high power in 30-second increments until it reaches 110°F to 115°F on an instant-read thermometer. Stir in the yeast and set aside to bloom until the mixture is bubbly and foamy, about 5 minutes.

Transfer the yeast mixture to the bowl of a stand mixer fitted with the paddle attachment or to a large bowl and add 2 cups of flour along with the salt. Mix until combined with the mixer or a wooden spoon. The mixture will be liquidy and lumpy at this point.

Add in another cup of flour and continue to mix, adding more flour in ¼-cup portions until the dough starts to pull away from the sides of the bowl. If using a stand mixer, switch to a dough hook attachment at this point. The dough should be soft and slightly sticky when you stop adding flour. Knead either in the mixer or by hand until the dough is elastic. By mixer, this will take about 5 minutes, and by hand it should take about 10 minutes. The dough may still be slightly lumpy but should spring back when you touch it.

MAKES 1 LOAF

1 cup whole milk

¾ cup water

3 tablespoons honey

2 tablespoons sugar

1 tablespoon butter, melted

1 teaspoon vanilla extract

2½ teaspoons active dry yeast

4 to 5 cups all-purpose flour

2½ teaspoons salt

Cooking spray

FOR THE SWIRL MIXTURE:

½ cup sugar

2 tablespoons ground cinnamon

3 tablespoons butter, melted

CONTINUED ON NEXT PAGE

CINNAMON SWIRL BREAD (CONTINUED)

Transfer the dough to a lightly oiled large bowl and cover with plastic wrap. Let the dough rise in a warm, draft-free spot by about one-third in size, which takes about 30 minutes for me; keep an eye on your dough size to avoid overproofing.

Grease a 9-inch loaf pan with cooking spray. Set aside. Using a rolling pin on a lightly floured surface, roll out your dough into a large rectangle. The shorter side should be about the same length as the length of your loaf pan.

To make the swirl mixture, in a small bowl, stir together the sugar and cinnamon.

Evenly sprinkle the swirl mixture all over the rolled-out dough, all the way to the edges. With your rolling pin, gently press the mixture into the dough. Starting on the loaf-pan-length side, use your hands to roll the dough into a tight log and place it seam-side down in the prepared loaf pan. Cover with plastic wrap and let the dough rest for about 15 minutes. Meanwhile, preheat your oven to 375°F. The dough will be just slightly puffed when ready to bake.

Brush the top of the loaf generously with some of the melted butter and bake until deep golden brown and when the inside reaches 195°F on an instant-read thermometer, 45 to 48 minutes.

Brush the remaining melted butter over the top of the loaf immediately when you take it out of the oven. Let the bread cool for about 20 minutes in the pan, and then turn out onto a cooling rack to finish cooling. Wait until the bread is completely cool to slice. Enjoy!

BAGELS

Homemade bagels are insanely good, and when you make them yourself, you can top them with all your favorite flavors! I suggest everything bagel spice blend, red pepper flakes, dried dill, or za'atar. Because they're first boiled and then baked, these bagels turn out with a crisp, bubbly outside and a super-chewy inside. They are the perfect breakfast all on their own or with your favorite bagel fillings. For a special treat, try them in my Bagel Strata (page 195).

MAKES 6 BAGELS

1½ cups warm water, approximately 100°F to 110°F

2¼ teaspoons active dry yeast

1 tablespoon sugar

3 tablespoons honey, separated

3¾ cups all-purpose flour, plus more for kneading

2 teaspoons salt

Cooking spray

1 egg

1 tablespoon water

Seasonings to top as desired (see note)

In the bowl of a stand mixer or in a large bowl, stir together the warm water, yeast, sugar, and 1 tablespoon of the honey. Let stand until foamy, 5 to 10 minutes.

Add 3½ cups of the flour and the salt, and mix together until a shaggy dough forms. If you are using a stand mixer, use the dough hook attachment to knead the dough until smooth and elastic, about 10 minutes. The dough should be pulling away from the sides of the bowl but sticking slightly to the bottom of the bowl as it kneads. If you're mixing by hand, turn the dough out onto a lightly floured work surface and knead by hand for about 15 minutes, adding the remaining ¼ cup flour if the dough is extremely sticky to the touch. The dough should still be slightly tacky. Place the dough in a lightly greased bowl and cover with plastic wrap. Let the dough rise in a warm, draft-free spot until it has almost doubled in size, 30 to 60 minutes. Lightly spray a baking sheet with cooking spray.

CONTINUED ON NEXT PAGE

BAGELS (CONTINUED)

Turn the dough out onto a clean work surface and divide it into 6 even portions. Using your hands and the work surface, shape each portion into a ball, then roll the seam side on your counter to seal it and to create a taught ball of dough. Next, use your fingers to press a hole into the center of each dough ball, and stretch it out to form your bagel shape. You'll want to make the holes a bit bigger than you think they need to be—they will close up as they rise and bake. Place each bagel onto the prepared baking sheet and cover with plastic wrap. Let stand until the bagels are just starting to look puffy, about 20 minutes. (Alternatively, you can also put the bagels into the fridge, and let them rise for about 4 hours.)

Line a large baking sheet with parchment paper and preheat your oven to 425°F. Fill a large, tall-sided skillet or pot with about 3 inches of water and stir in the remaining 2 tablespoons of honey. Bring the mixture to a low boil. Carefully add the bagels, in batches if necessary, to the boiling water and boil each bagel for about 30 seconds on each side. Using a large slotted spoon, transfer the bagels to the prepared baking sheet. Be careful—they will be a little puffy and slippery coming out of the boiling water.

In a small bowl, beat the egg with the water until well combined to make an egg wash. Generously brush each bagel all over with your egg wash. Then, top the bagels lightly or generously with your seasonings of choice. Bake the bagels until they reach a deep golden-brown color, 20 to 22 minutes. Let cool, split, toast, and enjoy!

EVERYTHING BAGEL SLIDER BUNS

These tiny rolls are topped with everything bagel seasoning,
and they make a perfect side to any breakfast. Plus, they're perfect for
breakfast sliders. They are the right size for just about anything
you need. See them in action in my Ham & Jam Sliders (page 175).

In a microwave-safe bowl, stir together the milk,
water, and sugar. Heat the mixture in the microwave
on high power in 30-second increments or until
the mixture reaches about 110°F on an instant-read
thermometer. Stir in the yeast and set aside to
bloom until the mixture is bubbly and foamy, about
5 minutes.

In the bowl of a stand mixer fitted with the paddle
attachment or in a large bowl, stir together the egg,
salt, and bloomed yeast mixture. Add the flour 1 cup
at a time, stirring between each addition, until all the
flour has been added and the mixture forms a shaggy
dough. Begin kneading the dough at this point, either
with a stand mixer or by hand until the dough is
smooth and stretchy, about 10 minutes. Then, knead
in the softened butter about 2 tablespoons at a time
until incorporated. It will take a good amount of
kneading to fully mix in each bit of butter—just keep
going! Lightly oil a large bowl and place the dough
inside the bowl. Cover with plastic wrap and let rise
until the dough has risen by about one-third, 20 to
30 minutes. Keep an eye on your dough—you do not
want to overproof it.

Lightly grease a 9-by-13-inch pan with canola oil and
preheat your oven to 375°F.

CONTINUED ON NEXT PAGE

MAKES 12 BUNS

1½ cups whole milk

¼ cup water

3 tablespoons sugar

2¼ teaspoons active dry yeast

1 egg

2 teaspoons salt

4 to 4½ cups all-purpose flour

5 tablespoons very soft butter

Canola oil for greasing

1 egg, lightly beaten

2 to 3 tablespoons everything bagel
    seasoning

Butter, cream cheese, or your favorite
    slider fillings for serving

EVERYTHING BAGEL SLIDER BUNS
(CONTINUED)

Divide the dough into 12 even sections by cutting it in half, each piece in half again, and each one of those pieces into thirds. Fold in any corners of each dough section to create a smooth, round top, and roll each section to create a ball. Evenly space the 12 dough balls on the prepared baking sheet, then cover. Let rise again until the balls have risen by about one-third, 10 to 15 minutes.

Brush the tops of the rolls generously with beaten egg and sprinkle the everything bagel seasoning generously over the top. Bake the rolls until they are a rich golden brown on top, 18 to 20 minutes.

Cool the rolls, then slice and enjoy with butter, cream cheese, or your favorite slider fillings.

GRUYÈRE-CHEDDAR BREAD

This bread is like a cheesy babka, and it's one of the yummiest things you can make. I love the combo of Gruyère and cheddar cheeses here, but you can use any other melting cheese that you like—pepper jack, provolone, and fontina would all be delicious options to twist up in this fluffy dough. Don't miss trying this for my Cheese Toast (page 153) or as an alternative ingredient in my Bagel Strata (page 195).

To make the flour paste, in a small saucepan, cook the milk and flour over medium heat, whisking constantly, until it forms a very thick paste. Set aside to cool.

To make the bread, in a microwave-safe bowl, stir together the milk and sugar. Heat in the microwave on high power in 30-second increments until the mixture reaches about 110°F on an instant-read thermometer. Stir in the yeast and let the mixture stand until it starts to look foamy and bubbly, about 5 minutes.

In the bowl of a stand mixer fitted with the dough hook or in a large bowl, stir together the egg and softened butter until the egg is lightly beaten. The butter will still have clumps, and that's ok! Add the yeast mixture, 2½ cups of the flour, the salt, oregano, and onion powder. Knead the mixture with the mixer or by hand until it is very elastic, smooth, and pulls away from the sides of the bowl, adding more flour if needed. This should take 15 to 20 minutes with the mixer or 20 minutes by hand.

CONTINUED ON NEXT PAGE

MAKES 1 LOAF

FOR THE FLOUR PASTE:

3 tablespoons whole milk

3 tablespoons all-purpose flour

FOR THE BREAD:

1 cup whole milk

3 tablespoons sugar

2¼ teaspoons active dry yeast

1 egg

¼ cup very soft butter, plus more for greasing

2½ to 3 cups all-purpose flour, plus more for rolling

2 teaspoons salt

2 teaspoons dried oregano

1 teaspoon onion powder

1 cup shredded Gruyère cheese

1 cup shredded cheddar cheese

GRUYÈRE-CHEDDAR BREAD (CONTINUED)

Place the dough back into the same bowl and cover with plastic wrap. Let the dough rise in a warm, draft-free spot until it has about doubled in size, which should take 30 to 45 minutes.

Lightly grease an 8-inch loaf pan with butter and set aside. Place the dough on a lightly floured surface. Using a rolling pin, roll out the dough into a large rectangle, with one side being a couple of inches longer than the length of your loaf pan. Evenly sprinkle the shredded Gruyère and cheddar cheeses all over the dough. Starting at the longer side, use your hands to roll the dough into a tight log. Using a long, sharp knife, slice the log lengthwise all the way down the log, and twist the two lengths of dough around each other into a swirl, with the open sides up. You want to get a lot of twists in here, so feel free to go pretty tight. Place the dough twist into the prepared pan and cover with plastic wrap. Let the dough rest until slightly puffed, about 20 minutes. Meanwhile, preheat your oven to 350°F.

Remove the plastic wrap and bake until the dough is golden brown on top and has reached about 190°F when tested with an instant-read thermometer, 55 to 60 minutes. Let cool for 10 minutes in the pan, and then turn it out onto a wire rack to finish cooling. Slice and enjoy!

CINNAMON BABKA

This recipe makes a fluffy, sticky, flavorful babka that is a true delight.
If you've never had a babka before, this should be the one you start with.
Babka is typically an enriched bread with a flavored filling
twisted all throughout, and it's a big fan fave in our house!

MAKES ONE LOAF

FOR THE BREAD:

¾ cup whole milk

¼ cup sugar

1 teaspoon vanilla extract

2¼ teaspoons active dry yeast

2 eggs

6 tablespoons very soft butter,
plus more for greasing

3 to 3½ cups flour, plus more for
rolling

½ teaspoon salt

FOR THE FILLING:

½ cup firmly packed brown sugar

1½ tablespoons ground cinnamon

⅛ teaspoon salt

5 tablespoons butter, melted

FOR THE SYRUP:

¼ cup water

⅓ cup sugar

⅛ teaspoon salt

½ teaspoon vanilla extract

To make the bread, heat the milk in the microwave on high power in 30-second increments until it reaches 115°F on an instant-read thermometer. Stir in the sugar, vanilla extract, and yeast. Let the mixture stand until it's bubbly and frothy, 5 to 10 minutes.

In the bowl of a stand mixer fitted with the dough hook or in a large bowl, stir together the eggs and soft butter—it will be a bit lumpy, but that's ok! Add the yeast mixture and stir to combine. Add 3 cups of the flour and the salt, and mix on medium speed with a dough hook attachment until a very soft dough forms, about 3 minutes. You can also stir this dough by hand with a wooden spoon for about 5 minutes. If the dough is still super sticky and wet, add a few more tablespoons of flour until it's pulling away from the sides of the bowl. Though soft, it should not stick to your fingers. Knead the dough with the mixer or by hand until it's very elastic and smooth, 5 to 8 minutes. Cover the bowl with plastic wrap and let the dough rise in a warm, draft-free spot until it's almost doubled in size, which takes 30 to 45 minutes in my kitchen.

To make the filling, in a small bowl, stir together the brown sugar, cinnamon, salt, and melted butter until well mixed. Set aside.

CONTINUED ON NEXT PAGE

CINNAMON BABKA (CONTINUED)

Grease an 8-inch loaf pan with a generous smear of butter and set aside. Using a rolling pin, roll out your dough on a lightly floured work surface into a large rectangle about ¼-inch thick. The shorter side of the dough should be a couple of inches longer than your loaf pan. Spread the filling evenly all over the dough, all the way to the edges. Using your hands, and starting at a long side, roll the dough up tightly into a log. Using a very sharp knife, slice the log in half lengthwise. Then, with the cut sides up, twist the dough around itself, keeping the cut sides of both pieces facing upward. Fold the whole twisted log in half and place it into the prepared loaf pan. Cover it in plastic and let the dough rest for about 20 minutes. Meanwhile, preheat your oven to 375°F.

Remove the plastic wrap and bake the babka until it registers about 175°F when tested with an instant-read thermometer, 40 to 45 minutes.

While the babka is baking, make the syrup. In a small saucepan, stir together the water, sugar, and salt, and bring the mixture to a boil over medium heat. Remove from the heat and let cool for 10 minutes. Stir in the vanilla extract.

When your babka comes out of the oven, immediately brush the top generously with the syrup mixture. Let the babka cool completely in the pan, and then turn it out to slice and serve.

FLOUR TORTILLAS

Making homemade tortillas is a therapeutic process of rolling and cooking an easy-to-make dough into fluffy, soft rounds. Trust me: these make burritos and tacos taste absolutely amazing, or you can eat them as a side to chili or Mexican-style dishes. It's so simple to make tortillas, and you probably already have everything you need to make them right now. Try them in my Breakfast Burritos (page 212) or Steak and Egg Tacos (page 211) and you'll thank me!

In the bowl of a stand mixer fitted with the dough hook attachment, stir together 2 cups flour, the salt, baking powder, oil, and water until a shaggy dough forms. Start mixing on medium speed, kneading the dough until soft and a little sticky, 5 to 6 minutes. It should pull away from the sides of the bowl, but may stick a little at the bottom. Add more flour if it's just a sticky mess at the bottom of your bowl. Cover the bowl with plastic wrap and let the dough rest for about 1 hour.

Line a rimmed baking sheet with parchment paper. For large tortillas (for burritos), divide the dough into 6 even sections; for small tortillas (for tacos), divide the dough into 10 even sections. Roll each piece of dough into a ball on a clean work surface. As you work, place the balls of dough on the prepared baking sheet and cover them with plastic wrap. Keep the dough balls covered at all times unless you are working with them.

MAKES 6 LARGE OR 10 SMALL TORTILLAS

2 to 2½ cups all-purpose flour, plus more for rolling

¾ teaspoon salt

¼ teaspoon baking powder

⅓ cup vegetable oil

⅔ cup warm water

CONTINUED ON NEXT PAGE

FLOUR TORTILLAS (CONTINUED)

Heat a large skillet over medium-high heat. On a lightly floured work surface, using a rolling pin, roll out one dough ball into a large circle (10 to 12 inches), or a small circle (about 6 inches), depending on the size you are making. It should be very thin at this point, so that you can almost see your fingers through it when you hold it up. Using your hands, gently transfer the tortilla to the skillet and cook until dark brown spots show on each side, about 30 seconds to 1 minute per side. Immediately place the cooked tortilla into a large resealable plastic bag and seal it. Repeat the process with the remaining dough balls, stacking the cooked tortillas on top of each other inside of the bag as and resealing it as you go. This helps the tortillas steam slightly and become soft throughout.

Serve warm.

SWEET LEMON TWISTS

These adorable little twists are super simple to make, but incredibly yummy to eat. Filled with sugar and lemon zest, they are just lightly lemony and appealingly sweet. Vary the citrus zest if you like—these would also be great with lime or orange zest for a change of pace.

MAKES 12 TWISTS

FOR THE ROLLS:

¾ cup whole milk

¼ cup sugar

1 teaspoon vanilla extract

2¼ teaspoons active dry yeast

2 eggs

¼ cup very soft butter

3 to 3½ cups all-purpose flour, plus more for rolling

½ teaspoon salt

FOR THE FILLING:

⅓ cup sugar

2 tablespoons finely grated lemon zest

¼ cup butter, at room temperature

To make the rolls, in a microwave-safe bowl, stir together the milk, sugar, and vanilla extract. Heat in the microwave on high power in 30-second increments until the mixture reaches 110°F to 115°F on an instant-read thermometer. Stir in the yeast and set aside until the mixture is foamy and bubbly, 5 to 10 minutes.

In the bowl of a stand mixer fitted with the dough hook attachment or in a large bowl, stir together the eggs and soft butter until the eggs are just beaten. The butter will still be in small chunks, and that's okay! Stir in the bloomed yeast mixture, 3 cups of the flour, and the salt and mix on medium speed, or using your hands in a large bowl, for several minutes, until a shaggy dough forms. Continue kneading with the mixer, or on a floured work surface by hand, adding flour as needed, until the dough is very smooth and elastic and is pulling away from the sides of the bowl. Leave the dough in the bowl and cover with plastic wrap. Let the dough rise in a warm, draft-free spot at room temperature until it has almost doubled in size. For me this takes 30 to 45 minutes.

To make the filling, in a small bowl, stir together the sugar and lemon zest. Using your fingers, rub the zest and sugar together for several minutes to release the oils and set aside.

CONTINUED ON NEXT PAGE

SWEET LEMON TWISTS (CONTINUED)

Line a large baking sheet with parchment paper. Turn out the dough onto a lightly floured work surface. Using a rolling pin, roll out the dough into a large rectangle that is about a ½-inch thick. On the short sides, trim away any uneven edges. Evenly spread the butter across the entire sheet of dough, and then sprinkle on the lemon zest and sugar mixture. Use your rolling pin to gently press the sugar into the butter and dough.

Next, slice the rectangle into 12 strips, ¾- to 1-inch wide. Fold each strip in half, sandwiching the filling on the inside. Then, twist each strip into a spiral, and twist each spiral into a roll, tucking the bottom of the roll underneath. Place each twisted roll onto the prepared pan, leaving about an inch of space between each roll. Cover with plastic wrap and let the rolls rise for about 20 minutes. Meanwhile, preheat your oven to 375°F.

Remove the plastic wrap from the rolls and bake until the rolls are lightly golden brown on top, 15 to 18 minutes. Let cool for 10 minutes on the pan before serving. These are best served warm!

ENGLISH MUFFINS

Homemade English muffins will forever ruin store-bought for you. They are super easy to make and they just take a little patience over the stove to cook. You'll end up with fluffy, chewy English muffins that are great on their own or as a breakfast sandwich. Try them in Sausage & Onion Breakfast Sandwiches (page 180), Avocado & Green Chile Breakfast Sandwiches (page 184), and Classic Eggs Benedict (page 192).

In a microwave safe bowl, stir together the milk, butter, sugar, and honey. Heat the mixture in the microwave on high power in 30-second increments until it reaches 110°F on an instant-read thermometer. Stir in the yeast and let the mixture stand until it becomes foamy and bubbly, about 5 minutes.

Pour the mixture into a large bowl and stir in the egg. Add the flour and salt and stir together until a shaggy dough forms with no dry pockets of flour. Form the dough into a rough ball in the bowl, cover, and let the dough rise in a warm, draft-free spot by about one-third in size, 30 to 45 minutes.

Sprinkle about half of the cornmeal onto a large sheet pan as evenly as possible and set aside. On a floured work surface, use a rolling pin to roll out the dough into a large rectangle, ½- to ¾-inch thick. Using a 3½-inch round cutter, cut out as many dough rounds as you can. You can gently re-knead the dough scraps and cut out more muffins one time. Put each round onto the prepared sheet pan, spacing them about an inch apart. Evenly sprinkle the remaining cornmeal on top of each dough round. Cover the sheet pan with plastic wrap, or another sheet pan inverted on top, and let the dough rest for 20 minutes.

MAKES 8 ENGLISH MUFFINS

1¾ cups whole milk

¼ cup butter

2 tablespoons sugar

1 tablespoon honey

2¼ teaspoon active dry yeast

1 egg

4 cups all-purpose flour, plus more for rolling

2 teaspoons salt

⅓ cup yellow cornmeal

Butter or jam for serving

CONTINUED ON NEXT PAGE

ENGLISH MUFFINS (CONTINUED)

Heat a large skillet or a griddle over low heat. Place
as many dough rounds as you can fit into the pan,
and cook or until they have puffed up and the bottoms
are dark golden brown, 8 to 10 minutes. Flip the
muffins and cook on the other side, 8 to 10 minutes
longer. Cool completely on a wire rack.

To serve, use a fork to gently split open the muffins.
Toast in a toaster or toaster oven until golden brown
on the inside, and smear with butter or jam!

SPICY MINI CORNBREADS

These spicy muffins are the perfect side to any breakfast. They are
filled with jalapeños and cayenne pepper to give a little kick to the
classic corn muffins you already know. I love eating these warm
from the oven with a little butter spread on top.

MAKES 12 MUFFINS

3 large jalapeño chiles

1 cup all-purpose flour

1 cup cornmeal

1½ teaspoons salt

1½ teaspoons baking powder

1½ teaspoons cayenne pepper

½ cup butter, at room temperature

2 tablespoons canola oil

½ cup sugar

¼ cup sour cream

3 eggs

Chop 2 of the jalapeños into small chunks, removing
the seeds. Slice the third jalapeño into thin, round
slices, leaving the seeds intact. Set aside.

In a bowl, stir together the flour, cornmeal, salt,
baking powder, and cayenne pepper. In a large bowl,
using a whisk, beat together the butter, oil, sugar,
and sour cream until well blended. Add the eggs one
at a time, beating well between each addition. Stir in
the flour mixture and the chopped jalapenos until
the mixture is well mixed and no dry pockets of flour
remain. Cover the bowl with plastic wrap and let the
batter rest for 20 minutes at room temperature.

Meanwhile, preheat your oven to 350°F and
generously grease a 12-cup muffin pan with cooking
spray, or line with paper liners. Divide the batter
evenly among the prepared muffin cups. They should
be pretty full. Top each muffin with a thin slice of
the remaining jalapeño. Bake the muffins until a
toothpick inserted in the center of a muffin comes
out clean, 16 to 18 minutes.

Let the muffins cool in the pan for 10 minutes, then
remove to a wire rack to finish cooling.

HERBY POPOVERS

Popovers are such an impressive yet easy thing to bake, and they're perfect for a fancy at-home brunch. These are best served warm from the oven and with a generous amount of butter or split open and piled high with soft scrambled eggs.

MAKES 6 POPOVERS

1¼ cups all-purpose flour

1 teaspoon salt

¼ teaspoon baking power

1¾ cups whole milk

4 eggs

½ cup finely chopped herbs (I like a mixture of chives, parsley, and thyme, but any herbs you prefer will work!)

Cooking spray

Butter for serving

In a small bowl, stir together the flour, salt, and baking powder. Set aside. In a large bowl, using a hand mixer on high speed, beat together the milk and eggs until frothy and a little thick, 5 minutes. Sift in the flour mixture and beat on high until well incorporated. Fold in the chopped herbs. Cover with plastic wrap and let the batter rest at room temperature for 1 hour.

Preheat your oven to 425°F. Place a 6-cup popover pan in the oven while it heats.

When the oven is hot, carefully pull the hot popover pan out of the oven and give the cups a generous coat of cooking spray. Working quickly, pour batter into each cup, filling it almost to the top. Bake for 15 minutes, then reduce the oven temperature to 350°F. Bake until the popovers are tall, puffed, and a deep golden-brown color, an additional 25 to 30 minutes.

Remove the popovers from the pan and serve as quickly as possible with butter.

BAKERY-STYLE TREATS

Sweets for breakfast are not a new concept, and I absolutely love eating something sweet with a cup of coffee in the morning or afternoon. This chapter is full of items like those you'd find in your local bakeshop, all customized for high-altitude. Whether you want beautiful and impressive cinnamon-scented morning buns, or a flavor-packed muffin or scone, there are no bad choices for a sweet breakfast treat.

If you know me, you know that breakfast cake is a food group in my own home! Every recipe in this section is perfect for breakfast in its own special way.

MAPLE PUMPKIN SCONES

I've always loved the combination of maple and pumpkin, and
these scones put them together in a fluffy, indulgent morning treat.
Maple extract really gives the icing that classic, donut-shop flavor.

MAKES 8 SCONES

3 cups all-purpose flour,
   plus flour for shaping

⅓ cup firmly packed brown sugar

1 tablespoon baking powder

1 teaspoon ground cinnamon

½ teaspoon ground ginger

½ teaspoon salt

¼ teaspoon ground nutmeg

6 tablespoons cold butter,
   cut into cubes

½ cup plus 2 tablespoons milk

⅓ cup prepared pumpkin puree

1 egg

1 tablespoon vanilla extract

FOR THE ICING:

1 cup powdered sugar

2 teaspoons water

1 teaspoon maple extract

⅛ teaspoon salt

To make the scones, in a large bowl, stir together
the flour, brown sugar, baking powder, cinnamon,
ginger, salt, and nutmeg. Using a pastry cutter or
clean hands, cut or press the cold butter into the
flour mixture until small, pea-sized bits of butter
are running throughout the mixture. In a bowl, stir
together the ½ cup milk, pumpkin puree, egg, and
vanilla extract. Pour the pumpkin mixture into the
flour mixture and stir together with a fork until a
dough begins to form.

Line a large baking sheet with parchment paper and
set aside. Turn the dough out onto a floured work
surface and gently knead together until you have a
fairly cohesive dough. Pat the dough into a circle that
is about 1 inch thick. Cut the circle into 8 wedges,
like you would cut a pizza, and place them evenly
spaced on the prepared baking sheet. Put the baking
sheet into the fridge and let the scones chill for about
30 minutes. Meanwhile, preheat your oven to 425°F.

Remove the scones from the fridge and brush the top
of each scone with the remaining 2 tablespoons milk.
Bake until the scones are golden brown and puffed
up on top, 10 to 12 minutes. Cool for 15 minutes
before icing.

To make the icing, whisk together the powdered
sugar, water, maple extract, and salt until you have a
smooth icing. Drizzle the scones generously with the
icing, and they're ready to eat!

VANILLA-EARL GRAY SCONES

These scones are lightly flavored with Earl Gray tea, and they make the perfect morning treat with your coffee or, well, tea! The foundation is hot milk into which the tea gets steeped to infuse its unique flavor throughout the scones.

To make the scones, in a microwave-safe bowl, heat ⅔ cup of the milk on high power until steaming, about 60 seconds. Add the tea bags and steep for 1 hour in the fridge.

Line a large baking sheet with parchment paper and set aside. In a large bowl, stir together the flour, sugar, baking powder, baking soda, and salt. Using a pastry cutter or clean hands, cut or press the cold butter into the flour mixture until small, pea-sized bits of butter are running throughout the mixture.

Remove the tea bags from the chilled milk, squeezing out any excess liquid. Stir in the sour cream, egg, and vanilla. Pour the sour cream mixture into the flour mixture and stir together with a fork.

Transfer the dough to a floured work surface and gently knead. Pat the dough into a circle about 1 inch thick, then cut the circle into 8 even wedges, and place them on the prepared pan. Chill the scones for about 30 minutes. Meanwhile, preheat your oven to 425°F.

Brush the scone tops with the remaining 2 tablespoons milk. Bake until the scones are golden brown and puffed, 10 to 12 minutes. Let cool for 15 minutes.

To make the icing, microwave the milk on high until very hot, 30 to 60 seconds. Add the tea bag and steep for 15 minutes. Remove the tea bag, squeezing the liquid into the bowl. Whisk in the sugar and salt. Drizzle the icing over the scones and serve.

MAKES 8 SCONES

FOR THE SCONES:

⅔ cup plus 2 tablespoons whole milk

3 Earl gray tea bags

3 cups all-purpose flour, plus flour for shaping

⅓ cup granulated sugar

1 tablespoon baking powder

¼ teaspoon baking soda

½ teaspoon salt

6 tablespoons cold butter, cut into cubes

3 tablespoons sour cream

1 egg

1 tablespoon vanilla extract

FOR THE ICING:

¼ cup whole milk

1 bag earl grey tea

1 cup powdered sugar

⅛ teaspoon salt

HONEY-WALNUT BISCOTTI

The combination of honey and walnuts is a perfect pair, and the crispness of these cookies makes them a good choice to dip in your morning cup of coffee. In my house, we go through these faster than I'd like to admit.

MAKES ABOUT 30 COOKIES

3½ cups all-purpose flour

½ teaspoon baking powder

½ teaspoon salt

½ cup canola oil

½ cup firmly packed brown sugar

½ cup honey

2 tablespoons milk

1 teaspoon vanilla extract

2 eggs

1 cup finely chopped walnuts

Preheat the oven to 350°F and line a large baking sheet with parchment paper.

In a bowl, stir together the flour, baking powder, and salt, and set aside. In the bowl of a stand mixer fitted with the paddle attachment or in a large bowl, beat together the canola oil, brown sugar, honey, milk, and vanilla extract until just combined. Beat in the eggs until incorporated. Slowly beat in the flour mixture. Finally, fold in the walnuts until well distributed. The dough will be very thick and sticky.

Form half of the dough into a long log on one side of the prepared baking sheet. Wet your hands and use them to shape the log fairly evenly. Repeat with the second half of the dough. Bake the logs until the dough has puffed and is firm to the touch, about 35 minutes. Cool the logs on the baking sheet until you can comfortably handle them, about 20 minutes.

Transfer one log to a cutting board and use a very sharp knife to cut the log at an angle into ½- to ¾-inch slices. Repeat with the second log of dough.

Place a fresh sheet of parchment on the baking sheet and lay the sliced cookies out onto the sheet. The cookies will not spread or puff; you should be able to fit all the cookies onto one baking sheet. Bake the cookie slices until golden brown around the edges and they feel very firm to the touch, 12 to 15 minutes. They will continue to firm as they cool. Let the cookies cool completely on the pan and enjoy!

SAVORY BISCUITS

These are a twist on classic biscuits with tons of savory flavors that will surprise you. Soy sauce gives them a deep color and flavor. I add black pepper and onion powder, but you can spice them with anything you'd like. I love them with a smear of cream cheese or just a pat of butter straight from the oven! Or, try them in my Bacon & Tomato Biscuit Sliders (page 183).

Line a large baking sheet with parchment paper and set aside. In a large bowl, stir together the flour, salt, black pepper, onion powder, sugar, baking soda, and baking powder. Using a pastry cutter or clean hands, cut or press the cold butter into the flour mixture until small bits of butter run throughout the entire mixture. Using a fork, stir in the ¾ cup buttermilk and the soy sauce until a shaggy dough forms.

Turn out the dough onto a floured work surface and gently knead the dough together. Using a rolling pin, roll out the dough into a long rectangle, and then fold it into thirds. Repeat the rolling and folding process two more times. Then, roll it out into a rectangle that is about 1 inch thick. Cut out biscuits with a 3-inch round cutter, rerolling and cutting the scraps if needed. Place the biscuits onto your prepared baking sheet and cover with plastic wrap. Put the baking sheet in the fridge and chill the biscuits for 30 minutes. Meanwhile, preheat your oven to 425°F.

Remove the biscuits from the fridge and brush the tops with the remaining 2 tablespoons buttermilk. Bake until the biscuits are tall, flaky, and deep golden brown on top, 10 to 12 minutes. Cool on the pan for 5 minutes before serving.

MAKES 6 BISCUITS

- 2½ cups all-purpose flour, plus flour for rolling
- 2 teaspoons salt
- 1 teaspoon freshly ground black pepper
- 1 teaspoon onion powder
- 1 teaspoon sugar
- 1 teaspoon baking soda
- 1 teaspoon baking powder
- ½ cup cold butter, cut into cubes
- ¾ cup plus 2 tablespoons buttermilk
- 2 tablespoons soy sauce

CREAM BISCUITS

Classic biscuits are easier to make than you might think, and you don't need any special equipment. Try them on their own or in Bacon & Egg Biscuit Sandwiches (page 179) and Biscuits with Bacon Gravy (page 188).

MAKES 12 TO 14 BISCUITS

4¼ cups all-purpose flour, plus flour for rolling

2 tablespoons sugar

2 tablespoons baking powder

2 teaspoons salt

1 cup very cold butter, cut into pieces

1½ cups cold heavy cream, plus 3 tablespoons for brushing

2 tablespoons honey

Line a large baking sheet with parchment paper. In a large bowl, stir together the flour, sugar, baking powder, and salt. Using a pastry blender, two forks, or clean hands, cut or press the cold butter pieces into the flour mixture until you have small chunks of butter about the size of peas running throughout the entire mixture. In a liquid measuring cup, stir together the 1½ cups heavy cream and the honey. Using a fork, gently stir the flour mixture as you pour in the cream mixture to form a lumpy dough.

Transfer the dough to a floured work surface and knead to form a ball. Add more flour if the dough is too sticky. Using a rolling pin, roll the dough into a rectangle 12 to 14 inches long and about 6 inches wide. Fold the dough into thirds. Repeat the rolling and folding process once more.

Roll the dough out a third time into a roughly round shape about ½-inch thick. Using the cutter of your choice—I use a 2½-inch square cutter—cut out biscuits from the dough. Stack and reroll dough scraps to cut out more biscuits, if desired.

Place the biscuits, evenly spaced, on your baking sheet. Cover with plastic wrap, and place in the fridge for about 30 minutes. Don't skip this step! While the biscuits chill, preheat your oven to 400°F.

Brush the biscuit tops with the remaining 3 tablespoons cream. Bake until puffy and golden brown, 13 to 15 minutes. Enjoy!

SAUSAGE & CHEDDAR MUFFINS

These umami-packed muffins are stuffed with crumbled sausage, sharp cheddar cheese, and caramelized onions, and they're seriously a meal all in one muffin! I love the flavor that cheddar gives, but you can swap out any cheese you prefer. Use any type of sausage you wish—pork, turkey, or chicken.

Slice the onion pole to pole into long slivers. Warm a skillet over medium heat. Add the olive oil and onion and cook, stirring often, until the onion is translucent, about 5 minutes. Reduce the heat to medium-low. Continue to cook the onion until soft and a light caramel color, 15 to 20 minutes. If your onion gets dry during the cooking process, add a tablespoon or so of water to help them stay moist. Remove the onion from the pan and set aside. Increase the heat to medium-high, add the sausage, and cook until crumbled, browned, and cooked through. Set aside to cool.

Preheat your oven to 425°F. Generously grease a 12-cup muffin pan with cooking spray or line it with paper liners.

In a large bowl, stir together the flour, baking powder, salt, and garlic powder. Using a pastry cutter or clean hands, cut or press in the cold butter until there are small bits of butter running throughout. Using a rubber spatula, stir in the milk until well blended. Then, fold in the cooked onion, sausage, and the cheese. The batter will be thick.

Divide the batter evenly among the muffin cups—the cups should be almost full. Bake until a toothpick comes out clean when inserted into the center and the tops are golden brown, 15 to 18 minutes. Let cool in the pan for 10 minutes before serving.

MAKES 12 MUFFINS

1 yellow onion

2 tablespoons olive oil

1 to 2 tablespoons water

½ pound bulk breakfast sausage

Cooking spray (optional)

2¼ cups all-purpose flour

2½ teaspoons baking powder

1½ teaspoons salt

1 teaspoon garlic powder

½ cup cold unsalted butter, cut into small pieces

1⅓ cups whole milk

4 ounces sharp cheddar cheese, shredded

MORNING BUNS

Morning buns are a fun take on cinnamon rolls. You can either make the pastry from scratch, or you can buy some (choose all-butter puff pastry). Either way, you'll end up with magically flaky, cinnamon-sugar-filled pastries. For best results, keep your butter in the freezer throughout the process until you use it.

MAKES 12 BUNS

FOR THE PUFF PASTRY:

1¾ cups all-purpose flour, plus more for rolling

1 tablespoon granulated sugar

½ teaspoon ground cinnamon

¼ teaspoon salt

1¼ cups grated frozen butter, kept frozen

¾ cup very cold water

FOR THE FILLING:

1½ cups granulated sugar

½ cup firmly packed brown sugar

2 tablespoons ground cinnamon

¼ teaspoon salt

Cooking spray (optional)

To make the puff pastry, in a large bowl, stir together the flour, sugar, cinnamon, and salt. Using a rubber spatula or wooden spoon, stir in ¼ cup of the frozen grated butter until evenly distributed. Slowly add in the cold water, stirring until the flour is completely incorporated and a dough begins to form. Turn the dough out onto a floured surface and knead once or twice to finish incorporating all the ingredients. The dough should be fairly soft and easy to work with.

Working quickly on a lightly floured surface, use a rolling pin to roll the dough into a large rectangle about 8 by 15 inches in size. Note that the size does not need to be perfect here. Arrange the dough so that a long side is facing you. Sprinkle half of the remaining frozen butter on the left two-thirds of the rolled-out dough. Fold the right side (without any butter) over the center of the dough and then fold once more into thirds to enclose the butter. Gently pinch the edges to lightly seal the dough. Roll out the dough again to the same size, reflouring your surface if needed, and repeat the butter sprinkling and folding process with the remaining frozen butter.

Once again, roll out the dough into a large rectangle, and fold into thirds, without any more butter (you should have used it all). Repeat the process two more times, for a total of 5 times rolling and folding.

CONTINUED ON NEXT PAGE

MORNING BUNS (CONTINUED)

Immediately wrap the dough in plastic wrap and pop it in the fridge for at least 30 minutes before using.

To make the filling, in a bowl, stir together 1 cup of the granulated sugar, the brown sugar, cinnamon, and salt. Set aside the remaining ½ cup granulated sugar in a bowl to use later.

To assemble, lightly grease a 12-cup muffin tin with cooking spray. Set aside. Remove the dough from the fridge and roll it out on a floured work surface into a large rectangle about 10 by 16 inches. Evenly sprinkle the filling mixture over the rectangle, all the way to the edges, and press it down into the dough with your hands, or with your rolling pin. Starting on the longer side of your rectangle, roll the dough into a tight spiral log. Wrap the dough tightly in plastic wrap and freeze for 30 minutes.

Remove the dough from the freezer and trim the edges of the log even. Then, cut the log into 12 equal slices: first cut the log in half; cut each of the halves in half; and then cut each remaining piece into thirds. Place each slice into a prepared muffin cup and place the pan in the fridge for 20 minutes. Meanwhile, preheat your oven to 400°F.

Take the rolls out of the fridge and place them directly into the preheated oven. Bake until golden brown from the top to the center, 20 to 25 minutes.

Immediately after you remove the buns from the oven, run a knife along the edges of each muffin cup to loosen, and remove them from the pan while hot—they will stick to the pan if not removed quickly. Let the buns cool for about 5 minutes, and then dip the tops into the remaining sugar. Enjoy warm!

DIRTY CHAI CINNAMON ROLLS

These rolls are flavored with Chai tea and espresso for a super
flavorful bite that reminds me of a favorite coffeehouse drink. There are
a lot of steps in making cinnamon rolls of any kind, but they are so
worth the work and I find the process almost calming. Plus, at the end,
you get a warm, gooey cinnamon roll. What could be better?

To make the rolls, in a microwave safe bowl, heat the milk on high power until just boiling, 1 to 2 minutes. Add the 4 tea bags and the espresso powder to the milk and let steep for 15 minutes.

Squeeze any excess liquid from the tea bags back into the bowl and discard the tea bags. Add the sugar and vanilla extract to the milk mixture and stir to combine. Test the temperature of the milk mixture with an instant-read thermometer—you want it to be 110°F to 115°F. Once it is, stir in the yeast, and let the mixture stand until frothy and bubbly, about 5 minutes.

In the bowl of a stand mixer fitted with the dough hook attachment or in a large bowl, stir together the eggs and soft butter. Next, stir in the bloomed yeast mixture. Add 4½ cups flour and the salt and mix on medium speed or knead the dough by hand on a floured surface until the dough is no longer sticky and pulls away from the sides of the bowl, adding more flour as needed, 3 to 4 minutes in a mixer, or 5 to 8 minutes by hand. Continue to knead until the dough is very elastic and smooth, 5 to 10 minutes. Place the dough back in the bowl if necessary, cover, and let it rise until just under doubled in size. For me, this takes 30 to 45 minutes.

MAKES 12 ROLLS

FOR THE DOUGH:

1⅔ cups whole milk

4 chai tea bags

2 teaspoons instant espresso powder

½ cup sugar

1 teaspoon vanilla extract

1 tablespoon active dry yeast

2 eggs

½ cup very soft butter

5 to 5½ cups all-purpose flour,
    plus flour for rolling

2 teaspoons salt

FOR THE FILLING:

Butter for greasing

1 cup firmly packed brown sugar

½ cup granulated sugar

3 tablespoons ground cinnamon

Leaves from 3 chai tea bags

2 teaspoons instant espresso powder

½ teaspoon salt

½ cup butter, softened

CONTINUED ON NEXT PAGE

DIRTY CHAI CINNAMON ROLLS (CONTINUED)

To make the filling, grease a 9-by-13 inch cake pan with butter and set aside. In a small bowl, stir together the brown sugar, granulated sugar, cinnamon, tea leaves, espresso powder, and salt.

On a floured surface, using a rolling pin, roll out the dough into a large rectangle that is about ½-inch thick. Spread the softened butter evenly all over the dough. Then, sprinkle the filling evenly over the top of the butter. Gently roll the rolling pin over the filling to press it into the dough. Starting on a long side, use your hands to roll up the dough into a tight log. Trim the edges of the log evenly. Then, cut the log into 12 equal slices: first cut the log in half; cut each of the halves in half; and then cut each remaining piece into thirds. Place the rolls cut-side down in the prepared cake pan, evenly spaced. Cover with plastic wrap and let the rolls rise for 20 minutes. Meanwhile, preheat your oven to 375°F.

Bake the rolls until golden brown all over, 14 to 16 minutes. Let cool for 5 minutes before frosting.

To make the frosting, steep the tea bag in the boiling water for 10 minutes, and then discard the tea bag. Let cool. In a bowl, whisk together the sour cream, powdered sugar, salt, and espresso powder. While whisking, slowly add the cooled tea until you reach a thick but easy to drizzle consistency.

Generously drizzle the frosting all over the rolls and enjoy!

FOR THE FROSTING:

1 chai tea bag

¼ cup boiling water

¼ cup sour cream

1½ cups powdered sugar

½ teaspoon salt

½ teaspoon instant espresso powder

FUNFETTI CRUMB CAKE

This is like your favorite coffee cake, birthday-cake style. Clear vanilla extract gives it just the right flavor. You can also use 1 teaspoon vanilla extract and ½ teaspoon almond extract to get a similar taste.

MAKES 8 SLICES

FOR THE CAKE:

Baking spray (or butter and flour) for greasing

½ cup butter, softened

½ cup granulated sugar

¼ cup sour cream

2 eggs

1 tablespoon clear vanilla extract

1 cup all-purpose flour

1½ teaspoons baking powder

½ teaspoon salt

⅓ cup rainbow sprinkles

FOR THE CRUMB TOPPING:

1 cup cake flour

½ cup granulated sugar

2 tablespoons firmly packed brown sugar

½ teaspoon baking powder

½ teaspoon salt

2 tablespoons rainbow sprinkles

¼ cup vegetable oil

1 tablespoon clear vanilla extract

Water, as needed

To make the cake, preheat the oven to 350°F. Grease an 8-inch round cake pan with baking spray and line the bottom with a parchment paper round, and a long strip of parchment paper that overhangs on each side for easy removal. Set aside.

In a large bowl, using an electric mixer on medium speed, beat together the butter, sugar, and sour cream until smooth. Beat in the eggs and vanilla until incorporated. Add the flour, baking powder, salt, and sprinkles and beat until well-blended and smooth. The batter will be thick. Spread the batter into the prepared pan and bake for 12 minutes.

To make the topping, in a bowl, combine the flour, both sugars, baking powder, salt, sprinkles, oil, and vanilla. Use a fork to stir all the ingredients together. If your crumb isn't quite coming together, add a teaspoon of water at a time until large crumbs form.

After the cake has baked for 12 minutes, remove it from the oven and evenly and gently sprinkle with the crumb topping. Return to the oven and bake until a cake tester inserted into the center comes out clean, 20 to 22 minutes.

Let the cake cool in the pan for 20 minutes. Then, run a knife around the edges, and use your parchment paper overhanging pieces to transfer it to a wire rack to finish cooling.

Use a sharp knife to cut the cake into slices and serve.

BANANA BREAD

Banana bread is one of the ultimate comfy food moments. This recipe
is super simple, and it works every single time. Tuck into a thick slice
of this easy banana bread and feel your stress melt away.
Don't forget to try it for Banana Bread French Toast (page 158), too!

Preheat your oven to 350°F and generously spray
an 8-inch loaf pan with cooking spray. Sprinkle
the bottom and all sides of the sprayed pan with
granulated sugar and shake out any excess. Set aside.

In a large bowl, using an electric mixer on medium
speed, beat together the ¾ cup sugar and the butter
until fluffy, about 2 minutes. Add the eggs, vanilla,
and mashed bananas and mix until incorporated.

In a bowl, stir together the flour, salt, baking soda,
and cinnamon. Add the flour mixture to the banana
mixture in 3 additions, mixing well between each
addition. Pour the batter into the prepared pan and
spread evenly. Bake until a toothpick inserted into the
center comes out clean, 60 to 65 minutes.

Let cool and enjoy!

MAKES 1 LOAF

Cooking spray for greasing

¾ cup sugar, plus more for sprinkling

6 tablespoons butter, softened

2 eggs

1 tablespoon vanilla extract

1½ cups mashed overripe bananas
(about 3 large bananas)

2 cups all-purpose flour

1 teaspoon salt

¾ teaspoon baking soda

½ teaspoon ground cinnamon

CINNAMON COFFEE CAKE

Cinnamon and sugar make this coffee cake the warmest, coziest, softest cake you've ever had. For me, there's nothing better than a sweet slice of breakfast cake with a cup of coffee, and this is the perfect cake.

MAKES 8 SLICES

FOR THE CAKE:

Baking spray (or butter and flour) for greasing

2½ cups all-purpose flour

1¼ teaspoons baking powder

1 teaspoon salt

1 cup butter, softened

1¼ cups granulated sugar

4 eggs

2 tablespoons milk

2 teaspoon vanilla extract

FOR THE SWIRL:

¼ cup firmly packed brown sugar

1 tablespoon ground cinnamon

1 tablespoon milk

FOR THE TOPPING:

3 tablespoon granulated sugar

1 teaspoon ground cinnamon

⅛ teaspoon salt

To make the cake, preheat your oven to 350°F. Generously grease an 8-inch round cake pan with baking spray and line the bottom of the pan with parchment paper.

In a bowl, stir together the flour, baking powder, and salt. In a large bowl, using an electric mixer on medium speed, beat together the butter and sugar until light and fluffy, about 2 minutes. Add the eggs, milk, and vanilla extract and beat until just combined. Add the flour mixture and mix until well incorporated and smooth, 2 to 3 minutes. Spread about two-thirds of the batter into your prepared pan.

To make the swirl, in a bowl, stir together the brown sugar, cinnamon, and milk until smooth.

Spread the swirl mixture all over the batter in your pan. Then, spread the remaining cake batter on top of that.

To make the topping, in a bowl, stir together the sugar, cinnamon, and salt. Sprinkle the mixture evenly over the top of the cake.

Bake the cake until a cake tester inserted into the center comes out clean, 52 to 55 minutes. Cool completely in the pan, then slice, and serve!

RAISED DOUGHNUTS

It took me a lot of time to develop a successful yeasted doughnut recipe that worked at a high altitude, but this one is the winner! These are fluffy, flavorful, and perfect when dipped into the icing or coating of your choice. Try the ones below or any of the icings from the Breakfast Tarts (page 169).

In a small, microwave-safe bowl, heat the milk and water on high power in 30-second increments until it reads 115°F on an instant-read thermometer. Mix in the sugar and yeast and set aside until the mixture is foamy and bubbly, about 5 minutes.

In the bowl of a stand mixer fitted with the dough hook attachment, mix together the eggs and the yeast mixture with a fork until just combined. Add the bread flour, ¾ cup of the all-purpose flour, and the salt. Mix on medium speed until a very sticky dough forms—it will stick to the sides, but should be very thick. If the mixture seems too wet, add a bit more flour—note that you don't want the dough to completely pull away from the sides of the bowl. Using the dough hook attachment, knead the dough on medium-low speed until the dough starts to pull away from the sides of the bowl, 5 to 10 minutes.

While mixing, add the butter 1 tablespoon at a time, letting it knead into the dough before each addition. This process can take a while, and you may need to scrape down the sides of the bowl to ensure that the butter gets fully incorporated. Increase the mixer speed to medium and knead the dough for an additional 10 to 15 minutes. Test the dough using the window pane test: pull off a small chunk of the dough and stretch it out between your fingers.

CONTINUED ON NEXT PAGE

MAKES 12 DOUGHNUTS & HOLES

⅓ cup whole milk

2 tablespoons water

3 tablespoons sugar

1 tablespoon active dry yeast

2 eggs

1 cup bread flour

¾ to 1½ cups all-purpose flour, plus more for rolling

1 teaspoon salt

4 tablespoons butter

4 to 5 cups canola oil

Cinnamon-Sugar Coating or Chocolate Icing (page 216)

It should stretch without breaking until it is so thin that you can almost see through it, like a window. Transfer the dough to a lightly oiled bowl and cover with plastic wrap. Let the dough rise in a warm, draft-free spot until it is about doubled in size. For me this takes about 30 minutes; it may be different in your kitchen.

Scrape the dough onto a generously floured work surface. It will still be fairly sticky at this point. Using a rolling pin, roll out the dough to about ½-inch thick. Cut the dough into your desired shapes using either a doughnut cutter, or a 2½-inch round cutter and a small ½- to 1-inch round cutter for the inside hole.

Line two large baking sheets with parchment paper, and a third baking sheet with several layers of paper towels. Arrange the cut doughnuts on the parchment-lined sheets and cover with plastic wrap. Let them rise until they spring back when touched, 10 to 15 minutes. Meanwhile, in a deep pot, heat about 4 cups canola oil until it reads 350°F to 375°F on a deep-frying thermometer.

A few at a time, carefully add the doughnuts to the hot oil and fry until deep golden brown, about 1 minute on each side. Use a slotted spoon or a metal skimmer to remove the fried doughnuts from the oil and place onto the paper towel-lined baking sheet to drain. Repeat to fry the remaining doughnuts.

Make your preferred coating, following the instructions on page 216. While the doughnuts are still hot, toss them in the cinnamon-sugar topping, if using, to coat fully. Transfer to the lined baking sheet to cool. If using the chocolate icing, drizzle it over the cooled doughnuts and serve.

STICKY BUNS

Sticky buns are a creative twist on classic cinnamon rolls. Instead of frosting, the rolls are baked in a sticky, nut-studded caramel sauce that drips all over when the rolls are tipped out of the pan. You may even love them more!

To make the buns, in a small saucepan, combine 3 tablespoons of the milk and 3 tablespoons flour. Stir constantly while heating over medium heat. Once the mixture turns into a very thick paste, about 1 to 2 minutes, remove the pan from the heat and let the mixture cool.

In a small microwave-safe bowl, stir together the remaining ¾ cup milk, the sugar, and vanilla. Heat on high power in the microwave in 30-second increments until the mixture reads 110°F to 115°F on an instant-read thermometer. Stir in the yeast, and let sit until foamy and bubbly, about 5 minutes.

In the bowl of a stand mixer fitted with the dough hook attachment or in a large bowl, stir together the egg and oil, and then stir in the bloomed yeast mixture. Add 2½ cups flour and the salt. Mix on medium speed or with your hands until the dough becomes very elastic and smooth, 10 to 12 minutes. If the dough is sticking to the sides of the bowl, add more flour until the dough pulls away from the sides easily. If you're kneading by hand, place the dough back into the large bowl and cover with plastic wrap. Let the dough rise in a warm, draft-free spot until just under doubled in size, 30 to 45 minutes.

While the dough is rising, make the filling: In a small bowl, stir together the brown sugar, granulated sugar, cinnamon, allspice, ginger, and salt, and set aside.

MAKES 8 BUNS

FOR THE BUNS:

¾ cup plus 3 tablespoons whole milk

2½ to 3 cups plus 3 tablespoons bread flour

3 teaspoons sugar

1 teaspoon vanilla extract

2¼ teaspoons active dry yeast

1 egg

¼ canola oil

1 teaspoon salt

FOR THE FILLING:

½ cup firmly packed brown sugar

2 tablespoons granulated sugar

1 tablespoon ground cinnamon

¼ teaspoon ground allspice

¼ teaspoon ground ginger

¼ teaspoon salt

CONTINUED ON NEXT PAGE

STICKY BUNS (CONTINUED)

FOR THE STICKY SAUCE:

Cooking spray

½ cup butter

½ cup firmly packed
   dark brown sugar

¼ cup light corn syrup

1 teaspoon vanilla extract

¼ teaspoon salt

1 cup chopped pecans or walnuts

¼ cup butter, softened

To make the sticky sauce, lightly grease an 8-inch round cake pan with cooking spray and set aside. In a small saucepan over medium-low heat, melt the butter, brown sugar, corn syrup, vanilla extract, and salt, stirring constantly. Once the butter has fully melted and the mixture is smooth, remove from the heat and pour the mixture into the prepared pan. Evenly sprinkle the nuts on top of the sticky mixture.

Using a rolling pin, on a lightly floured work surface, roll out the dough into a large rectangle about ¼-inch thick. Spread the softened butter evenly all over the dough, leaving a ¼-inch border around the edges. Sprinkle the filling mixture all over the butter. Use your rolling pin to gently press the filling into the butter, which will make it easier to roll up. Starting on a long side, use your hands to roll the up the dough into a tight log. Trim off the edges with a sharp knife, and then cut the log into 8 even rolls. Arrange the rolls cut-side down on top of the sticky sauce in the prepared cake pan. Cover with plastic wrap and let the rolls rise for about 20 minutes. Meanwhile, preheat your oven to 375°F.

Remove the plastic wrap and cover the pan tightly with foil. Place the pan of buns onto a large baking sheet to catch any spills. Bake for 35 minutes.

Remove the foil and bake until the buns are golden brown all over, 20 minutes more. Let the buns cool in the pan for 3 to 5 minutes. Use oven mitts to carefully invert the pan onto a large plate, and then lift the pan off the buns. Your sticky sauce should spill all over the buns. Be sure to enjoy them warm!

LEMON-WALNUT BUNDT CAKE

This is the perfect breakfast cake. If you're not in the habit of eating cake for breakfast, now is certainly the right time to start. This one is glazed while it's still warm, which creates a lightly crisp, lemony exterior that I'm obsessed with!

To make the cake, preheat the oven to 350°F. Grease a 12-cup Bundt pan well with baking spray.

In the bowl of a stand mixer fitted with the paddle attachment, or in a large bowl, stir together the flour, sugar, baking powder, lemon zest, and salt. Set aside 1 tablespoon of the flour mixture. In a bowl, stir together the oil, eggs, and milk until just mixed. With the mixer running on low speed, slowly pour the egg mixture into the flour mixture and mix until completely incorporated and smooth, 3 to 4 minutes. Fold in the lemon juice until just incorporated. Toss the chopped walnuts with the reserved flour mixture and then fold them into the batter until the walnuts are well distributed throughout. Pour the batter into the prepared pan, spreading evenly, and bake until a cake tester inserted in the center comes out clean, 52 to 55 minutes.

While the cake bakes, make the glaze: In a small bowl, whisk together the lemon juice, powdered sugar, and salt until smooth. The glaze will be fairly thin.

Let the cake cool for 15 minutes in the pan, and then turn it out onto a serving plate or cake stand. Use a wooden or metal skewer to poke deep holes all over the cake. Use a brush to generously glaze the entire cake several times over, using all of the glaze mixture—it's going to seem like a lot. Just keep brushing it all over until you've used everything, and then let the cake finish cooling. Slice and serve.

MAKES ONE LARGE BUNDT CAKE

FOR THE CAKE:

Baking spray (or butter and flour) for greasing

3 cups all-purpose flour

1¾ cups granulated sugar

1¾ teaspoons baking powder

2 tablespoons finely grated lemon zest

1 teaspoon salt

¾ cup canola oil

4 eggs

¾ cup whole milk

¼ cup fresh lemon juice

1 cup finely chopped walnuts

FOR THE GLAZE:

½ cup fresh lemon juice

1 cup powdered sugar

Pinch of salt

CHOCOLATE CAKE DOUGHNUTS

The sour cream in these doughnuts gives them a craggy, cracked top that gets crunchy when it fries and holds on to the icing perfectly. Cake-style doughnuts are my favorite kind, and these chocolate ones are super simple, and delicious.

MAKES 12 TO 15 DOUGHNUTS & HOLES

FOR THE DOUGHNUTS:

3 cups all-purpose flour, plus more for rolling

1 cup granulated sugar

½ cup Dutch process cocoa powder

2½ teaspoons baking powder

½ teaspoon baking soda

¼ teaspoon espresso powder

½ teaspoon salt

1 cup sour cream

½ cup butter, melted

3 eggs

1 tablespoon vanilla extract

4 to 5 cups vegetable oil

FOR THE ICING:

2 cups powdered sugar

2 to 3 tablespoons water

1 teaspoon vanilla extract

To make the doughnuts, in a large bowl, stir together the flour, sugar, cocoa powder, baking powder, baking soda, espresso powder, and salt until well blended. In a bowl, stir together the sour cream, melted butter, eggs, and vanilla extract until smooth. Pour the egg mixture into the flour mixture and stir together using a silicone spatula until a wet, sticky dough forms.

On a floured piece of parchment paper, use a rolling pin to roll out the dough until it is about ¾-inch thick and cover with another piece of parchment paper. Slide the whole sheet onto a large baking sheet and wrap with plastic wrap. Put the baking sheet in the fridge and chill for 2 hours before frying.

When you're ready to fry, heat the oil in a deep pot over medium-high heat until it reaches 360°F on a deep-frying thermometer. Pull out the chilled dough and cut into doughnut shapes using a doughnut cutter, or a large round and a small round cutter.

In batches, add the doughnuts to the hot oil and fry until puffed and cracked all over, 1 to 2 minutes per side. Using a large slotted spoon or a metal skimmer, transfer the fried doughnuts to a wire rack set over paper towels to drain and cool before icing.

To make the icing, whisk together the powdered sugar, 2 tablespoons water, and the vanilla, adding more water if needed to reach a thick but drizzle-able consistency. Dip your doughnuts in the glaze, and let the glaze drizzle over the doughnut as it sets.

VANILLA CRANBERRY GRANOLA

Granola is so easy to make, and you can make it with anything you have on hand or that sounds good. This one is studded with macadamia nuts and dried cranberries, and it's filled with crispy rice cereal for a crunch.

Preheat your oven to 300°F. Have a large, clean, rimmed baking sheet ready to go.

In a large bowl, stir together the oats, rice cereal, macadamia nuts, brown sugar, and salt. In a bowl, whisk together the honey, oil, egg white, and vanilla extract. Pour the oil mixture into the oats mixture and stir until the ingredients are completely coated. This might take a few minutes but take your time—you really want everything well coated.

Spread the granola mixture evenly on the baking sheet. Bake until lightly golden, stirring once, about 30 minutes. Remove from the oven and let cool completely in the pan. The granola may seem like it's still soft when it comes out of the oven, but it will crisp up as it cools.

When the granola mixture is cool, use your fingers to break it up into the desired size pieces. Add the cranberries and toss well. Store in an airtight container until ready to serve. Enjoy!

MAKES 4 CUPS GRANOLA

3 cups old-fashioned oats

1 cup crispy rice cereal

½ cup chopped macadamia nuts

½ cup firmly packed brown sugar

1 teaspoon salt

⅓ cup honey

¼ cup canola oil

1 egg white

1 tablespoon vanilla extract

¾ cup chopped dried cranberries

DARK CHOCOLATE RUGELACH

Rugelach takes a little extra effort, but it's one of the yummiest
little treats you can make. These are great to set out at the end of
a celebratory brunch, or with a quick cup of coffee in the morning.

MAKES 70 TO 72 COOKIES

FOR THE RUGELACH:

2¼ cups all-purpose flour

½ teaspoon salt

8 ounces cold cream cheese,
   cut into cubes

1 cup cold unsalted butter,
   cut into cubes

2 teaspoon vanilla extract

1 egg yolk

FOR THE FILLING:

6 ounces dark chocolate,
   roughly chopped

4 tablespoons butter

⅓ cup powdered sugar

2 tablespoons Dutch process
   cocoa powder

¼ teaspoon salt

¼ teaspoon espresso powder

To make the rugelach, in a large food processor, pulse together the flour and salt. Add the cream cheese and butter and pulse until crumbly. Add the vanilla and egg yolk and pulse until a cold, fairly sticky dough forms.

Divide the dough into 3 even sections. Roll each section between 2 pieces of parchment into a large round about ⅛-inch thick. Slide the rounds onto a large baking sheet—you can stack them—and refrigerate for at least 1 hour.

To make the filling, in a small saucepan, melt together the chocolate and butter over low heat. Remove from the heat and stir in the powdered sugar, cocoa powder, salt, and espresso powder until smooth.

Place 1 dough round on a work surface. Spread one-third of the filling over the dough all the way to the edges. Use a long knife to cut the round into 24 thin wedges. Pull a wedge out, and starting from the thick side, roll it up tightly into a spiral. Set aside on a small baking sheet. Repeat with all the wedges. Freeze the spirals for at least 30 minutes before baking. Repeat with the remaining dough and filling.

Preheat the oven to 375°F and line a large baking sheet with parchment paper. Arrange the frozen rugelach on the prepared baking sheet, leaving 2 inches between each one, and bake until they are golden brown and flaky, 18 to 20 minutes. Let cool on a wire rack and enjoy!

BAKEWELL CRUMB CAKE

When my friend Merickson introduced me to Bakewell tarts and *The Great British Bake Off* television show, I was immediately obsessed. This flavor combo works with any kind of baked dish, and coffee cake is no exception.

To make the cake, preheat your oven to 350°F, and generously grease an 8-inch square cake pan with baking spray.

In a large bowl, stir together the flour, sugar, almond flour, baking powder, and salt. In a bowl, stir together the egg, buttermilk, oil, and almond extract. Pour the egg mixture into the flour mixture and stir together with a rubber spatula until well blended. Pour about half of the cake batter into the prepared cake pan and spread it evenly.

To make the filling, put the jam in a small bowl and heat on high heat for 30 to 40 seconds, or until warmed through.

Spread the warm cherry jam on top of the cake batter. Dollop the remaining cake batter all over the jam and then spread it evenly across the top.

To make the crumb topping, in a bowl, using a fork, stir together the flour, almond flour, brown sugar, melted butter, oil, and almond extract until large crumbs form.

Sprinkle the crumbs evenly all over the top of the cake, using all of the crumb mixture. Bake the cake until a cake tester inserted into the center comes out fairly clean, with just some cherry jam sticking to it, 30 to 34 minutes. Let the cake cool completely in the pan before slicing and serving.

MAKES ONE 8-INCH CAKE

FOR THE CAKE:

Baking spray (or butter and flour) for greasing

1½ cups all-purpose flour

½ cup granulated sugar

¼ cup almond flour

1 teaspoon baking powder

½ teaspoon salt

1 egg

⅔ cup buttermilk

2 tablespoons oil

2 teaspoons almond extract

FOR THE FILLING:

½ cup cherry jam

FOR THE CRUMB TOPPING:

¾ cups all-purpose flour

½ cup almond flour

½ cup firmly packed brown sugar

¼ cup butter, melted

2 tablespoons canola oil

1 teaspoon almond extract

ORANGE POUND CAKE

This is a twist on a classic pound cake and is another perfect option for breakfast cake. Mashing up sugar with orange zest creates a flavorful, crunchy topping that I'm totally addicted to, and it takes this cake to the next level.

MAKES 1 LOAF

Baking spray (or butter and flour) for greasing

FOR THE SUGAR CRUST:

2 tablespoons finely grated orange zest

3 tablespoons sugar

FOR THE POUND CAKE:

2¾ cups all-purpose flour

1¼ teaspoons baking powder

1 teaspoon salt

1 cup butter, softened

1¼ cups sugar

4 eggs

3 tablespoons finely grated orange zest (from 1 to 2 oranges)

¼ cup fresh orange juice (from about 1 orange)

Preheat your oven to 350°F. Generously grease a 9-inch loaf pan with baking spray and set aside.

To make the sugar crust, in a small bowl, use your fingers to mash the orange zest into the sugar. Do this for about 1 to 2 full minutes, which will allow the oils to really mix with the sugar. Cover and set aside.

To make the cake, in a bowl, stir together the flour, baking powder, and salt. Set aside. In a large bowl, using an electric mixer, beat together the butter and sugar until fluffy, 2 to 3 minutes. Add the eggs, one at a time, mixing well between each addition. Add the orange zest and juice and mix well. While mixing, slowly add the flour mixture and mix until smooth. The batter will be thick.

Pour the batter into the prepared loaf pan and spread evenly. Generously sprinkle sugar crust over the top of the batter. Bake until a cake tester inserted into the center of the cake comes out clean, about 1 hour and 10 minutes.

Let cool completely in the pan before removing and slicing. Enjoy!

CHOCOLATE CHUNK MUFFINS

These muffins are super simple to make, but taste like they are complicated. I've recently started letting muffin batter rest for at least 30 minutes before baking, and it helps to create a super tall, domed muffin top that will make your homemade muffins resemble a bakery's.

In a large bowl, stir together the flour, sugar, almond flour, baking powder, and salt. In a bowl, stir together the milk, melted butter, eggs, and vanilla extract until well blended. Pour the egg mixture into the flour mixture and fold together until almost mixed, but some pockets of flour remain. Then, add the chopped chocolate and stir until fully mixed and no flour pockets remain. Cover the batter with plastic wrap and let stand at room temperature for 30 to 45 minutes.

Preheat your oven to 400°F. Generously grease a 12-cup muffin tin, or line the cups with paper liners.

Divide the batter evenly among the muffin cups—they will be fairly full. Sprinkle the tops with the coarse sugar and bake until golden brown and a toothpick inserted into the center of a muffin comes out clean, 18 to 20 minutes.

Let the muffins cool and enjoy!

MAKES 12 MUFFINS

2¾ cups all-purpose flour

1 cup granulated sugar

¼ cup almond flour

1¾ teaspoons baking powder

1 teaspoon salt

½ cup whole milk

½ cup butter, melted

2 eggs

2 teaspoons vanilla extract

6 ounces dark chocolate, chopped

3 tablespoons coarse sugar

APPLE CAKE

This fluffy yellow cake is topped with thinly sliced apples and flavored with a little bit of lemon juice. It's got subtle flavors that I'm crazy about and the batter comes together easily. The method for mixing the cake may seem odd, but trust me, it works perfectly! I like slices dolloped with whipped cream.

MAKES ONE 8-INCH CAKE

Cooking spray

½ cup butter, softened

½ cup sugar

2 eggs

¼ cup sour cream

2 tablespoons plus 1 teaspoon fresh lemon juice

1 teaspoon vanilla extract

1 cup all-purpose flour

1¼ teaspoons baking powder

½ teaspoon salt

2 green apples

Preheat your oven to 350°F and generously grease an 8-inch cake pan with cooking spray, and line the bottom with parchment paper.

In a large bowl, combine the butter, sugar, eggs, sour cream, 2 tablespoons of the lemon juice, the vanilla, flour, baking powder, and salt. Using an electric mixer, mix together until just blended—the mixture will be thick and fairly smooth. Pour the batter into the prepared cake pan and set aside.

Peel and core the apples, then slice them thinly. Toss the sliced apples with the remaining 1 teaspoon lemon juice. Arrange the apple slices over the top of the cake in a fan shape, spreading them evenly. Bake the cake until a cake tester inserted into the center of the cake comes out clean, 40 to 42 minutes. Let cool completely in the pan before slicing and serving.

CARROT CAKE MUFFINS

These muffins are topped with a swirl of cream cheese topping that gives them that full-on carrot cake feeling. I've always been a proponent of cake for breakfast, and we all know that a good muffin just tastes like cake.

In a large bowl, stir together the flour, brown sugar, baking powder, salt, cinnamon, and ginger. In a small bowl, stir together the oil, milk, eggs, and vanilla extract until incorporated. Pour the egg mixture into the flour mixture and stir together with a silicone spatula. Add the shredded carrots, stirring until completely incorporated. Cover the bowl with plastic wrap and let the mixture stand at room temperature while your oven preheats, about 20 minutes. Meanwhile, preheat your oven to 400°F and line the cups of a 12-cup muffin pan with paper liners.

To make the topping, in a small bowl, whisk together the cream cheese, powdered sugar, and vanilla extract.

Divide the batter evenly among the prepared muffin cups. The batter should come almost to the tops of the cups, so don't worry if they look super full! Dollop small spoonfuls of the cream cheese topping on top of the batter and use a toothpick to swirl it into the batter. Bake the muffins until a toothpick inserted into the center of a muffin comes out clean, 15 to 18 minutes.

Let the muffins cool completely and enjoy!

MAKES 12 MUFFINS

2 cups all-purpose flour

½ cup firmly packed brown sugar

1¾ teaspoons baking powder

1 teaspoon salt

1 teaspoon ground cinnamon

½ teaspoon ground ginger

¾ cup vegetable oil

¼ cup milk

2 eggs

1 teaspoon vanilla extract

1½ cups shredded carrots

FOR THE CREAM CHEESE TOPPING:

6 ounces cream cheese,
   at room temperature

¼ cup powdered sugar

1 teaspoon vanilla extract

APPLE-OAT MUFFINS

These apple and oat muffins are the perfect combination of fruit, spices, and muffin. It's a whole breakfast all in one, as the oats with the apples create a pretty filling little morning treat.

MAKES 12 MUFFINS

1 Granny Smith apple

2¼ cups all-purpose flour

½ cup firmly packed brown sugar

2 teaspoons baking powder

1 teaspoon ground cinnamon

½ teaspoon ground nutmeg

¼ teaspoon ground allspice

½ teaspoon salt

1 cup milk

½ cup vegetable oil

2 teaspoons vanilla extract

2 eggs

Cooking spray (optional)

½ cup old-fashioned oats

Peel, core, and chop the apple into small chunks (about ½-inch).

In a large bowl, stir together the flour, brown sugar, baking powder, cinnamon, nutmeg, allspice, and salt. In a small bowl, stir together the milk, vegetable oil, vanilla extract, and eggs until well combined. Pour the egg mixture into the flour mixture along with the chopped apples and use a silicone spatula to mix until just combined and no dry pockets of flour remain. Cover the batter and let it stand for 30 minutes at room temperature. Meanwhile, preheat your oven to 400°F and generously grease a 12-cup muffin pan with cooking spray or line it with paper liners.

Fold the oats into the rested batter until incorporated. Divide the batter evenly among the muffin cups—the cups will be fairly full. Bake until the muffins are golden and puffed, and a cake tester inserted into the center of a muffin comes out clean, 18 to 20 minutes.

Let the muffins cool completely before serving.

BLACKBERRY RICOTTA CAKE

Ricotta makes cake devilishly special. It seems fluffy and simple,
but it creates a texture and flavor that really can't be matched.
This cake is packed with fresh blackberries and topped
with coarse sugar for a crunchy topping that you'll love.

Preheat your oven to 350°F. Generously grease an
8-inch round cake pan with baking spray and line the
bottom with parchment paper.

In a large bowl, whisk together the flour, sugar,
baking powder, and salt. In a bowl, whisk together
the eggs, ricotta, melted butter, and vanilla extract.
Stir the egg mixture into the flour mixture until
almost combined, but some of the dry mixture is still
dry. Add in the blackberries, and stir together until
incorporated and no more dry streaks remain.

Pour the batter into your prepared cake pan and
smooth evenly with a spoon. Sprinkle the raw sugar
on top. Bake until a toothpick inserted into the center
of the cake comes out clean, 45 to 50 minutes. Let cool
completely in the pan.

When cool, gently remove the cake from the pan and
cut into slices to serve.

MAKES ONE 8-INCH CAKE

Baking spray (or butter and flour)
  for greasing

1¾ cups all-purpose flour

1 cup granulated sugar

1¾ teaspoons baking powder

1 teaspoon salt

3 eggs

1½ cups whole-milk ricotta cheese

½ cup butter, melted

1 teaspoon vanilla extract

1 cup fresh blackberries

2 tablespoons raw sugar

WAFFLES & PANCAKES

Waffles and pancakes are always a winner when it comes to breakfast dishes. I've put together some simple recipes for these breakfast staples, and I've also thrown in some really indulgent ones like Blueberry Cheesecake Pancakes and Birthday Cake Waffles for something special. Fair warning: it's going to be hard to choose!

BASIC WAFFLES

These classic waffles are fluffy, flavorful, and crisp. I love to use waffles
instead of bread for breakfast sandwiches, or eat them on their own
with syrup, whipped cream, and strawberries. No matter how
you like them, waffles are a welcome breakfast treat.

In a large bowl, stir together the flour, ¼ cup of the
brown sugar, the baking powder, and salt. Set aside.
In a small bowl, stir together the milk, butter, and
vanilla extract. Set aside.

In another bowl, using an electric mixer on medium-
high speed, beat together the eggs and the remaining
1 tablespoon brown sugar until the mixture is very
thick, fluffy, and pale, about 5 minutes. Stir the
reserved milk mixture into the flour mixture until
just incorporated. Then, gently fold in the beaten
egg mixture until completely incorporated. Let the
batter rest, covered, at room temperature for about
30 minutes. Meanwhile, preheat your waffle iron
according to the manufacturer's instructions.

Spray the grates of the waffle iron with cooking
spray and cook the waffles according to the
manufacturer's instructions. I use a high heat
setting, and cook the waffles until deep golden brown,
5 to 6 minutes. Enjoy with your favorite toppings!

MAKES 8 TO 10 WAFFLES

2 cups all-purpose flour

¼ cup plus 1 tablespoon firmly
    packed brown sugar

2½ teaspoons baking powder

1 teaspoon salt

1½ cups whole milk

6 tablespoons butter, melted

2 teaspoons vanilla extract

2 eggs

Cooking spray

BIRTHDAY CAKE WAFFLES

Whether it's your birthday, or for no reason at all, these
waffles are a dream. The frosting is addictive, and
who doesn't want sprinkles first thing in the morning?

MAKES 8 TO 10 WAFFLES

FOR THE WAFFLES:

2 cups all-purpose flour

¼ cup plus 1 tablespoon
  granulated sugar

2½ teaspoons baking powder

1 teaspoon salt

1½ cups whole milk

¼ cup canola oil

2 teaspoons vanilla extract

½ teaspoon almond extract

2 eggs

¼ cup sprinkles

Cooking spray

FOR THE FROSTING:

2 tablespoons sour cream

2 tablespoons whole milk,
  or as needed

1 teaspoon vanilla extract

½ teaspoon almond extract

¼ teaspoon salt

2 cups powdered sugar,
  plus more if needed

In a large bowl, stir together the flour, ¼ cup of the
granulated sugar, the baking powder, and salt, and
set aside. In a small bowl, stir together the milk, oil,
and vanilla and almond extracts. Set aside.

In another bowl, using an electric mixer on high
speed, beat together the eggs and remaining
1 tablespoon granulated sugar until the mixture is
very thick, fluffy, and pale, about 5 minutes. Stir the
reserved milk mixture into the flour mixture until
just incorporated. Then, gently fold in the beaten
egg mixture until completely incorporated. Let the
batter rest, covered, at room temperature for about
30 minutes. Meanwhile, preheat your waffle iron
according to the manufacturer's instructions.

When you're ready to cook, fold the sprinkles into
the batter. Spray the grates of the waffle iron with
cooking spray and cook the waffles according to the
manufacturer's instructions. I use a high heat setting,
and cook the waffles until deep golden brown, 5 to
6 minutes.

To make the frosting, in a bowl, whisk together the
sour cream, milk, vanilla extract, almond extract,
salt, and powdered sugar until smooth. The icing
should be thick, but you should be able to drizzle
it. Add more milk or powdered sugar to reach your
desired consistency. Drizzle it generously over your
waffles and serve!

PUMPKIN WAFFLES

I'm one of those people who loves all things pumpkin flavored,
and waffles are the perfect place for this favorite flavor to shine.
These waffles have the warm spices and pumpkin puree you know
and love, and they are fluffy on the inside and crisp on the outside.

In a large bowl, stir together the flour, ¼ cup of the brown sugar, the baking powder, cinnamon, ginger, allspice, and salt. Set aside. In a small bowl, stir together the milk, pumpkin puree, oil, and vanilla extract, and set aside.

In another bowl, using an electric mixer on high speed, beat together the eggs and the remaining 1 tablespoon brown sugar until the mixture is very thick, fluffy, and pale, about 5 minutes. Stir the reserved milk mixture into the flour mixture until just incorporated. Then, gently fold in the beaten egg mixture until completely incorporated. Let the batter rest, covered, at room temperature for about 30 minutes. Meanwhile, preheat your waffle iron according to the manufacturer's instructions.

Spray the grates of the waffle iron with cooking spray and cook the waffles according to the manufacturer's instructions. I use a high heat setting, and cook the waffles until deep golden brown, 5 to 6 minutes. Serve with whipped cream, cinnamon, and syrup.

MAKES 8 TO 10 WAFFLES

2½ cups all-purpose flour

¼ cup plus 1 tablespoon firmly packed brown sugar

2½ teaspoons baking powder

1 teaspoon ground cinnamon, plus more for serving

1 teaspoon ground ginger

¼ teaspoon ground allspice

1 teaspoon salt

1 cup whole milk

One 15-ounce can prepared pumpkin puree

¼ cup canola oil

2 teaspoons vanilla extract

2 eggs

Whipped cream and syrup for serving

CARROT CAKE WAFFLES

One of the best things about waffles and pancakes is that you can flavor them to taste like all your favorite cakes. I actually think these waffles are better than carrot cake, and the icing gives them that classic cream-cheese-frosting feeling.

MAKES 8 TO 10 WAFFLES

2 cups all-purpose flour

3 tablespoons firmly packed brown sugar

2 teaspoons baking powder

2 teaspoons ground cinnamon

1 teaspoon baking soda

1 teaspoon salt

½ teaspoon ground ginger

½ teaspoon ground nutmeg

½ cup canola oil

1 cup buttermilk

2 eggs

1 teaspoon vanilla extract

1½ cups freshly shredded carrots

¼ cup chopped pecans, plus more for serving, if desired

Cooking spray

FOR THE ICING:

4 ounces cream cheese, softened

¼ cup butter, softened

1½ cups powdered sugar

2 to 3 tablespoons milk

1 teaspoon vanilla extract

In a large bowl, stir together the flour, brown sugar, baking powder, cinnamon, baking soda, salt, ginger, and nutmeg. In a small bowl, stir together the oil, buttermilk, eggs, and vanilla extract. Pour the egg mixture into the flour mixture and stir until just incorporated. Fold in the carrots and pecans. Cover the batter with plastic wrap and let it rest for 20 minutes. Meanwhile, preheat your waffle iron according to the manufacturer's instructions.

Spray the grates of the waffle iron with cooking spray and cook the waffles according to the manufacturer's instructions. I use a high heat setting, and cook the waffles until deep golden brown, 5 to 6 minutes.

To make the icing, in a bowl, whisk together the cream cheese, butter, powdered sugar, 2 tablespoons milk, and vanilla extract. The icing should be thick, but you should be able to drizzle it, so add more milk if needed. Generously drizzle your pancakes with the icing and serve with more pecans if you'd like.

CHERRY-ALMOND WAFFLES

Cherry and almond are a top-tier flavor combination, and they are a perfect pair to enhance your waffles. Almond waffles topped with a luscious cherry syrup are one of the most tempting brunch dishes that you can make at home.

To make the cherry syrup: In a saucepan, stir together the cherries, sugar, cornstarch, salt, water, and lemon juice. Cook over medium heat, stirring frequently, until thick, 5 to 8 minutes. Cover and set aside until ready to serve.

To make the waffles, in a large bowl, stir together the flour, almond flour, sugar, baking powder, and salt. In a small bowl, stir together the eggs, milk, vanilla extract, and almond extract. Pour the egg mixture into the flour mixture and stir until just incorporated. Then, stir in the melted butter. Let the batter rest at room temperature for 20 minutes. Meanwhile, preheat your waffle iron according to the manufacturer's instructions.

Spray the grates of the waffle iron with cooking spray and cook the waffles according to the manufacturer's instructions. I use a high heat setting, and cook the waffles until deep golden brown, 5 to 6 minutes. Serve with the cherry syrup.

MAKES 8 TO 10 WAFFLES

FOR THE CHERRY SYRUP:

2 cups pitted fresh cherries or thawed frozen cherries

2 tablespoons sugar

1 tablespoon cornstarch

⅛ teaspoon salt

¼ cup water

1 tablespoon fresh lemon juice

FOR THE WAFFLES:

1½ cups all-purpose flour

½ cup almond flour

¼ cup sugar

1 tablespoon baking powder

½ teaspoon salt

2 eggs

1½ cups whole milk

1 teaspoon vanilla extract

1 teaspoon almond extract

½ cup butter, melted

BASIC BUTTERMILK PANCAKES

Pancakes of all kinds are what I think of when I imagine a big Saturday morning breakfast. This is a classic buttermilk pancake recipe, and it's the perfect base for all kinds of toppings and add-ins. For example, try popping 5 to 8 blueberries or chocolate chips into each pancake before baking. These also serve as the base for Lime Pie Pancakes (page 133) and Blueberry Cheesecake Pancakes (page 134).

MAKES 8 TO 10 LARGE PANCAKES

2 cups all-purpose flour

¼ cup sugar

2 teaspoons baking powder

1 teaspoon salt

1½ cups buttermilk

1 egg

1 tablespoon vanilla extract

¼ cup butter, melted

2 to 3 tablespoons butter, plus butter for serving

Syrup for serving

Preheat the oven to the lowest setting (that's 170°F for me), if desired. Heat a large skillet over medium heat.

In a large bowl, stir together the flour, sugar, baking powder, and salt. In a small bowl, stir together the buttermilk, egg, and vanilla extract. Pour the buttermilk mixture into the flour mixture, and stir together until just mixed, but some lumps remain. Fold in the melted butter until fully incorporated.

Add a small pat of butter to the hot pan to melt. In batches, add about ⅓ cup batter per pancake to the hot pan, spacing them evenly. Cook until golden brown, 1 to 2 minutes on each side. Transfer the cooked pancakes to a plate and, if desired, keep warm in the oven while you cook the rest of the batter.

Serve with your favorite syrup and more butter!

CORNMEAL PANCAKES

These are by far my favorite pancakes. They sound simple, but they are an incredible twist on a classic pancake with a subtle, sweet corn flavor. You can top these with maple syrup and butter, but the maple whipped cream is seriously delightful. Don't forget to try these with the Breakfast Corn Dogs (page 138).

To make the pancakes, in a large bowl, stir together the flour, cornmeal, sugars, baking powder, baking soda, and salt. In a bowl, whisk together the eggs, buttermilk, and melted butter. Add the egg mixture to the flour mixture and use a rubber spatula to stir everything together—some lumps are okay! Cover and let the batter rest at room temperature for 20 minutes.

Preheat a large skillet or a griddle over medium heat. If desired, preheat the oven to its lowest setting (that's 170°F for me). Set a wire rack in a baking sheet.

Add a small pat of butter to the heated pan. Using a ladle or a large spoon, drop ¼ to ⅓ cup of batter onto the pan. Add as many pancakes to the pan as will fit. Cook the pancakes until you notice small bubbles start to pop up on the surface and the bottom edge is golden brown, 2 to 3 minutes. Using a large spatula, gently flip the pancakes and cook until golden on the bottom, about 2 more minutes. If desired, transfer the pancakes to the rack set inside the baking sheet, and place in the warm oven while you continue cooking. Continue to cook the remaining batter, melting more butter in the pan before each batch.

To make the maple whipped cream, beat the cream until soft peaks form. Add the maple syrup and salt and continue beating until you have stiff peaks.

To serve, divide the pancakes among serving plates, top with the maple whipped cream, and enjoy!

MAKES 8 LARGE PANCAKES

FOR THE PANCAKES:

1⅔ cups all-purpose flour

½ cup cornmeal

½ cup granulated sugar

¼ cup firmly packed brown sugar

½ teaspoon baking powder

¼ teaspoon baking soda

1 teaspoon salt

2 eggs

1½ cups buttermilk

½ cup butter, melted

4 to 5 tablespoons cold butter
    for cooking

FOR THE MAPLE WHIPPED CREAM:

1½ cups heavy cream

⅓ cup pure maple syrup

⅛ teaspoon salt

VEGAN CHOCOLATE PANCAKES

You won't miss the eggs or dairy in these super-chocolatey pancakes. The chocolate chunks running throughout make these pancakes delicious without any toppings, but I like mine with whipped coconut cream on top. Sliced strawberries, chocolate syrup, and powdered sugar are wonderful topping options, too. Vegan butter is a plant-based butter, and I love the flavor of avocado- and olive oil-based butters. Look for coconut whipped cream in the frozen section and vegan butter near the margarine at your grocery store.

MAKES 8 TO 10 PANCAKES

1½ cups all-purpose flour

½ cup almond flour

¼ cup unsweetened Dutch process
    cocoa powder

¼ cup firmly packed brown sugar

2 teaspoons baking powder

½ teaspoon salt

3 ounces dark chocolate,
    chopped

1¾ cups almond milk
    (or any nut milk)

3 tablespoons vegetable oil

1 teaspoon vanilla extract

2 to 3 tablespoons vegan butter

Coconut whipped cream to top

In a large bowl, stir together the flour, almond flour, cocoa powder, brown sugar, baking powder, and salt. Add the chocolate and toss to coat it in the flour mixture. In a small bowl, stir together the almond milk, vegetable oil, and vanilla extract. Pour the almond milk mixture into the flour mixture and stir until just incorporated and no dry pockets remain. The batter should still be slightly lumpy.

Preheat the oven to its lowest setting (that's 170°F for me), if desired. In a large skillet, melt about ½ tablespoon of vegan butter over medium-low heat. In batches, add about ⅓ cup of batter per pancake to the hot pan, spacing them evenly. Cook until you notice bubbles popping up on top of each pancake, 2 to 3 minutes. Flip and cook until puffed, and no longer jiggly when you shake the pan, 2 to 3 minutes more. Transfer the cooked pancakes to a plate and, if desired, keep warm in the oven while you cook the rest of the batter.

Serve the pancakes with your toppings of choice.

LIME PIE PANCAKES

These pancakes are like eating a slice of a refreshing lime pie, and I'm so here for that! Cooking a crumb topping right into the pancake creates a crunchy topping reminiscent of pie crust, and a generous dollop of lime curd gives it that tart flavor we all know and love. This is a fancy pancake dish that's perfect for a leisurely brunch.

Prepare the lime curd and pancake batter as directed.

To make the crumb topping, in a small bowl, using a fork, stir together the melted butter, flour, powdered sugar, granulated sugar, and salt until the mixture is crumbly.

To make the whipped topping, using an electric mixer, beat together the heavy cream and powdered sugar until it forms stiff peaks. Beat in the sour cream until incorporated. Cover and chill until ready to serve.

Preheat the oven to its lowest setting (that's 170°F for me), if desired. Warm a large skillet over medium heat and melt a small pat of butter in the pan.

In batches, add ½ to ¾ cup of the batter per pancake into the buttered pan, spacing them evenly. Generously sprinkle the top of each pancake with the crumb topping. Cook until bubbles form on top, 1 to 2 minutes. Flip the pancakes and cook until golden on the bottom, 1 to 2 minutes more. Transfer the cooked pancakes to a plate and, if desired, keep warm in the oven while you cook the rest of the batter.

To serve, divide the pancakes among serving plates. Top each cooked pancake with a generous dollop of lime curd, an extra sprinkle of the crumb topping, and a spoonful of whipped topping. Enjoy!

MAKES 6 TO 8 LARGE PANCAKES

1 batch Lime Curd (page 216)

1 batch Basic Buttermilk Pancakes (page 126)

FOR THE CRUMB TOPPING:

4 tablespoons butter, melted

½ cup all-purpose flour

½ cup powdered sugar

¼ cup granulated sugar

⅛ teaspoon salt

FOR THE WHIPPED TOPPING:

1 cup heavy cream

3 tablespoons powdered sugar

2 tablespoons sour cream

Butter for cooking

BLUEBERRY CHEESECAKE PANCAKES

These are some seriously indulgent pancakes! Layering the creamy
cheesecake filling with fluffy pancakes and a rich blueberry syrup
is the perfect way to enjoy cheesecake for breakfast. You can
swap in any fresh berries that you prefer here—blackberries,
chopped strawberries—even cherries would be amazing!

MAKES 8 TO 10 PANCAKES

FOR THE BLUEBERRY TOPPING:

1 pint fresh blueberries

¼ cup sugar

1 tablespoon fresh lemon juice

1 tablespoon cornstarch

⅛ teaspoon salt

2 to 3 tablespoons water

FOR THE CHEESECAKE FILLING:

8 ounces cream cheese, softened

½ cup sugar

1 teaspoon vanilla extract

1 batch Basic Buttermilk Pancakes
(page 126)

Butter for cooking

To make the blueberry topping, in a small saucepan,
stir together the blueberries, sugar, lemon juice,
cornstarch, and salt. Cook the mixture over medium
heat, stirring often, until the mixture becomes bubbly
and thick, 8 to 10 minutes. Remove the pan from the
heat and stir in 2 tablespoons water. If the mixture is
too thick to drizzle, add another tablespoon of water.
Keep warm.

To make the cheesecake filling, in a bowl, whisk
together the cream cheese, sugar, and vanilla until
smooth. Cover and set aside.

Prepare the pancake batter as directed.

Preheat the oven to its lowest setting (that's 170°F for
me), if desired. Heat a large skillet over medium heat,
and melt a small pat of butter in the pan. In batches,
add about ⅓ cup batter per pancake to the hot pan,
spacing them evenly. Cook until golden brown, 1 to
2 minutes on each side. Transfer the cooked pancakes
to a plate and keep warm in the oven while you cook
the rest of the batter.

To serve, divide the pancakes among serving plates.
Layer each pancake with the cheesecake filling and
then top the with the warm blueberry topping. Enjoy!

OATMEAL APPLE PANCAKES

These pancakes are hearty and piled high with spicy, sweet apples.
They have the perfect combination of spices, and the apples create
a syrupy topping that I'm obsessed with. There's no wrong way
to enjoy pancakes, but this cozy version is a great place to start.

To make the apple topping, peel and core the apples and cut them into small chunks. In a saucepan, stir together the apples, brown sugar, cinnamon, lemon juice, water, and salt. Cook over medium heat until the apples are soft and the sauce is boiling and slightly thickened, 8 to 10 minutes. Remove from the heat and set aside.

To make the pancakes, in a large bowl, stir together the flour, oats, sugar, baking powder, salt, and cinnamon. In a small bowl, stir together the milk, egg, vanilla extract, and oil. Pour the egg mixture into the flour mixture and stir together until incorporated, but some lumps still remain.

Heat a large skillet over medium heat. If desired, pre-heat the oven to its lowest setting (that's 170°F for me).

Add a small pat of butter to the heated pan and tilt the pan to coat it evenly. Pour about ⅓ cup of the batter onto the pan and use a spoon to spread it gently into about a 3-inch round. Add as many pancakes to the pan as will fit. Cook the pancakes until golden brown on each side, 2 to 3 minutes per side. Transfer the cooked pancakes to a plate and keep warm in the oven while you cook the rest of the batter.

To serve, divide the pancakes among serving plates. Top with a helping of apples and sauce and enjoy!

MAKES 8 TO 10 PANCAKES

FOR THE APPLE TOPPING:
2 large Granny Smith apples
¼ cup firmly packed brown sugar
1½ teaspoons ground cinnamon
2 tablespoons fresh lemon juice
2 tablespoons water
⅛ teaspoon salt

FOR THE PANCAKES:
1¾ cups all-purpose flour
¾ cup old-fashioned oats
¼ cup sugar
2 teaspoons baking powder
1 teaspoon salt
1 teaspoon ground cinnamon
1½ cups whole milk
1 egg
1 tablespoon vanilla extract
¼ cup canola oil
2 to 3 tablespoons butter

BREAKFAST CORN DOGS

Think about a breakfast sausage link wrapped up in pancake batter
and fried. Yeah, I'm drooling too. I used the cornmeal pancake
batter here to give it a similar vibe to a corn dog,
but breakfast-style! Use any type of sausage that you like.

**MAKES ABOUT 14 SMALL
CORN DOGS**

1 batch Cornmeal Pancakes
(page 129)

2 tablespoons all-purpose flour

One 12-ounce package uncooked
sausage links

5 to 6 cups canola oil, for frying

Pure maple syrup for serving

Prepare the cornmeal pancakes as directed, adding
the additional 2 tablespoons flour to the flour mixture.

Next, heat a large skillet over medium heat, and add
the sausage links. Cook the sausages until browned
on all sides, about 10 minutes. Let the sausages cool
before proceeding.

In a large, deep pot, heat the oil over medium-
high heat until it reaches 375°F on a deep-frying
thermometer. Line a large baking sheet with paper
towels for draining and set aside.

When you're ready to fry, in batches, dip the cooled
sausage links into the cornmeal pancake batter to
coat completely, letting the excess batter drip back
into the bowl. Carefully slide the sausages into the oil
and fry until golden brown all over, 3 to 4 minutes.
Using tongs, remove the corn dogs from the hot oil and
place on the prepared baking sheet to drain and cool.
Repeat to batter and fry the remaining sausage links.

Serve the corn dogs warm with syrup for dipping.

DUTCH BABY WITH STONE FRUIT

Dutch babies are super tasty and really beautiful. They're an easy way to make a showstopper breakfast because of how tall and grand they get while baking. I love this macerated stone fruit topping, but the Dutch baby is also great with berries or even Nutella.

To make the stone fruit topping, peel and pit the peach and plum, and slice them into fairly thin slices. In a small bowl, toss the sliced fruit with the lemon juice, sugar, and salt. Cover the bowl with plastic wrap and let the mixture stand for at least 10 minutes and up to 1 hour before serving.

To make the Dutch baby, put a 10-inch cast-iron skillet in your oven and preheat the oven to 450°F. In a large bowl, with an electric mixer on medium-high speed, beat the eggs until very foamy and pale, 3 to 5 minutes. Add the milk and vanilla and beat well. In a small bowl, sift together the flour, sugar, and salt. While mixing, slowly add the flour mixture to the eggs and mix until incorporated.

Using oven mitts, carefully pull the preheated skillet out of the oven and put the butter in it immediately. Once the butter has melted, pour in the batter and quickly return the pan to the oven. Bake until the Dutch baby is tall and puffed all around the edges and a deep golden brown, 16 to 18 minutes.

To serve, slice the Dutch baby like a pie and top each piece with a spoonful of the stone fruit topping. Be sure to enjoy this while it's warm.

MAKES 1 LARGE DUTCH BABY

FOR THE STONE FRUIT TOPPING:

1 large fresh peach

1 large fresh plum

1 tablespoon fresh lemon juice

1 tablespoon sugar

⅛ teaspoon salt

FOR THE DUTCH BABY:

3 eggs

⅔ cup whole milk

1 tablespoon vanilla extract

⅔ cup all-purpose flour

1 tablespoon sugar

½ teaspoon salt

5 tablespoons butter

SAVORY DUTCH BABY

Dutch babies are already such a bold, beautiful, and yummy breakfast dish, but this savory version is on another level. I love the combination of flavors with salsa and avocado on top, and it's such a unique way to enjoy the puffy oven pancake.

MAKES 1 DUTCH BABY

3 eggs

⅔ cup whole milk

⅔ cup all-purpose flour

1 tablespoon sugar

1 teaspoon salt

1 teaspoon freshly ground black pepper

1 teaspoon ground cumin

3 tablespoons freshly grated Parmesan cheese

1 ripe avocado, thinly sliced

¼ cup prepared salsa

Put a 10-inch cast-iron skillet in your oven and preheat the oven to 450°F. In a large bowl, beat the eggs with an electric mixer on medium-high speed until very foamy and pale, 3 to 5 minutes. Add the milk and beat well. In a small bowl, sift together the flour, sugar, salt, black pepper, and ground cumin. While mixing the egg mixture, slowly add the flour mixture until incorporated. Stir in the Parmesan cheese.

Using oven mitts, carefully pull the preheated skillet out of the oven and put the butter in it immediately. Once the butter has melted, pour in the batter and quickly return the pan to the oven. Bake until the Dutch baby is tall and puffed all around the edges and a deep golden brown, 16 to 18 minutes.

To serve, top with the sliced avocado and the salsa, then cut into wedges.

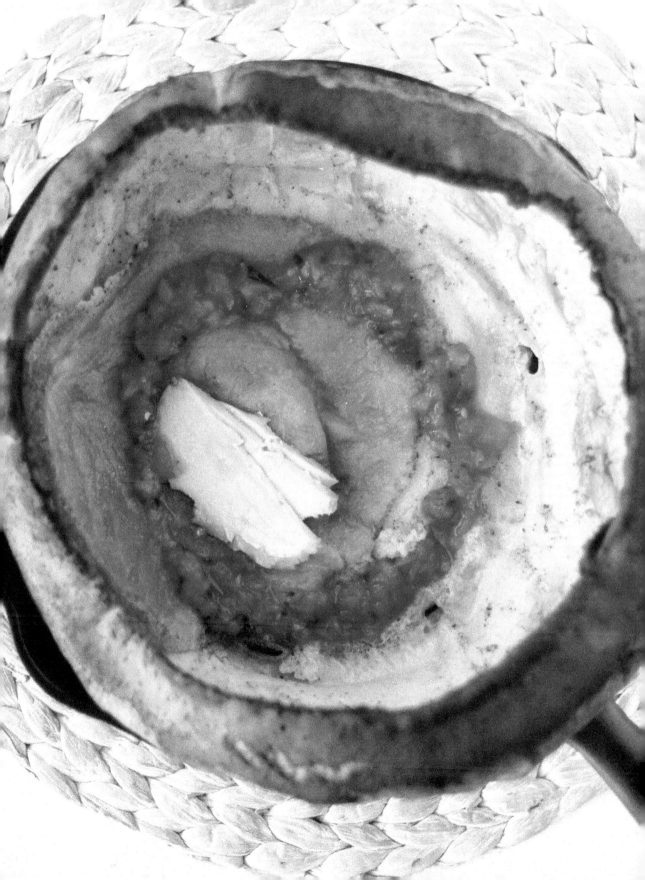

TOASTS

We're not talking about your ordinary buttered toast here, guys—we're talking about cheese toast, all kinds of French toasts, and toasts made on homemade, super flavorful bread!

My favorite thing about this chapter is that you get to use the amazing homemade breads you learned in the first chapter and turn them into super yummy treats—there's Banana-Chocolate Toast (on the Chocolate Chunk Cranberry Bread), French Toast Dippers (made with Brioche), Strawberry Toast (made with the Cinnamon Swirl Bread), and much more. This section will show you all the wonderful ways to use that fresh baked bread that you successfully created in your high-altitude kitchen.

STRAWBERRY TOAST

This is a super creative way to use your Cinnamon Swirl Bread.
This toast is a combination of several bold flavors, and the results
are complex and delicious. Try it for an easy weekday morning breakfast.

MAKES 4 SLICES

4 slices Cinnamon Swirl Bread
  (page 33)

4 ounces soft cream cheese

2 tablespoons powdered sugar

1 teaspoon vanilla extract

5 to 6 strawberries, sliced

1 to 2 teaspoons honey

½ teaspoon freshly ground
  black pepper

Toast the bread slices in a toaster until golden brown.
Transfer the toast to a work surface.

In a small bowl, stir together the cream cheese,
powdered sugar, and vanilla extract until smooth.
Divide the cream cheese mixture among the 4 slices
of toast, spreading evenly. Top each slice with a
layer of sliced strawberries, a drizzle of honey, and
a sprinkle of black pepper.

Serve right away!

CARAMELIZED ONION & EGG TOAST

Thick, toasted slices of white bread topped with soft scrambled eggs and caramelized onions make the perfect quick yet filling breakfast. You can make this with Gruyère-Cheddar Bread (page 41) for an even more savory dish.

Slice the onion pole-to-pole into long slivers. In a skillet, heat the olive oil over medium heat. Add the onion and cook, stirring often, until caramelized, 15 to 20 minutes. Add 1 to 2 tablespoons water as the onion cooks to help keep it moist. Set the onion aside.

In a small bowl, beat the eggs with generous pinches of salt and pepper until well blended. In a small skillet over low heat, warm the canola oil. Add the eggs and cook, stirring constantly, until soft and scrambled. Keep warm.

Toast the bread in a toaster until light golden brown and divide among serving plates. Top each piece of toast with a generous pile of eggs and some of the caramelized onion. Serve right away.

MAKES 4 SLICES

½ large yellow onion

1 tablespoon olive oil

1 to 2 tablespoons water

6 eggs

1 tablespoon canola oil

Salt and freshly ground black pepper to taste

4 slices Basic White Bread (page 21)

BANANA-CHOCOLATE TOAST

Here's another simple but flavor-packed dish—all you do is take toasted
Chocolate Chunk Cranberry Bread and top it with chocolate hazelnut
spread and sliced bananas, and add a dash of salt and sugar on top.
The salt brings out the flavor and makes this toast super yummy!

MAKES 4 SLICES

4 thick slices Chocolate Chunk
  Cranberry Bread (page 29)

¼ cup chocolate-hazelnut spread

2 large, ripe bananas, sliced

1 teaspoon sugar

½ teaspoon salt

Toast the bread slices in a toaster until golden brown.
Transfer the toast to a work surface.

Divide the chocolate-hazelnut spread among the
4 slices of toast, spreading evenly. Top each slice with
a layer of sliced bananas. Sprinkle each piece with
sugar and salt, dividing evenly, and serve right away.

CHEESE TOAST

Don't let the simplicity of this dish fool you: this simple, cheese-topped toast tastes incredible! I like to use the oven's broiler setting so you get a nice contrast between the crispy-crunchy top and soft inside and bottom of the bread slices.

Arrange the oven rack in the middle of your oven, about 12 inches away from the heat source, and turn on your oven's broiler to the high setting and line a large baking sheet with foil. Lightly spray the foil with cooking spray.

Arrange the bread slices on the sheet pan. Divide the shredded cheese evenly among the bread slices, piling it up. Place the bread under the broiler and cook until the cheese is toasted and bubbling, 2 to 3 minutes. Remove the pan from the oven and immediately sprinkle with the black pepper. Enjoy!

MAKES 4 SLICES

Cooking spray

4 thick slices of Gruyère-Cheddar Bread (page 41)

½ cup finely grated sharp cheddar cheese

1 teaspoon freshly ground black pepper

PUMPKIN FRENCH TOAST

I'm so here for all-pumpkin-all-the-time recipes, so here's another breakfast dish that you can't resist if you love pumpkin. Make it with the sweet version of my pumpkin bread, and you're in for a spicy, fall-filled treat!

MAKES 8 TO 10 SLICES

1 sweet loaf Pumpkin Bread (page 27)

5 eggs

2 egg yolks

½ cup whole milk

¼ cup firmly packed brown sugar

1 teaspoon vanilla extract

½ teaspoon ground cinnamon

½ teaspoon ground ginger

¼ teaspoon salt

¼ cup cold butter

Pure maple syrup for serving

Preheat the oven to the lowest setting (that's 170°F for me), if desired. Put a wire rack inside a rimmed baking sheet and set aside.

Slice the loaf into slices about 1-inch thick and set them out on the work surface.

Heat a large skillet or griddle over medium heat. In a wide, shallow bowl, whisk together the eggs, egg yolks, milk, brown sugar, vanilla extract, cinnamon, ginger, and salt.

Melt a small pat of butter on the pan for each slice of French toast. In batches, gently press the bread slices into the egg mixture and let the mixture soak in, about 20 seconds on each side. Remove the bread slices from the egg mixture, letting the excess drip back into the bowl, and add it to the buttered pan. Cook until golden brown on each side, 2 to 3 minutes per side. Transfer to the rack and keep warm in the oven while you cook the rest of the bread.

Serve warm with maple syrup.

CHOCOLATE-CRANBERRY FRENCH TOAST

This is a super decadent, chocolaty French toast made with homemade chocolate-cranberry bread. The berries in the bread give a little tartness to each bite, and the chocolate in the bread melts as you cook it, which everyone will love.

Preheat the oven to the lowest setting (that's 170°F for me), if desired. Put a wire rack inside a rimmed baking sheet and set aside.

Cut the loaf into thick slices and set them out on the work surface.

Heat a large skillet or a griddle over medium heat. Meanwhile, in a wide, shallow bowl, whisk together the eggs, egg yolks, milk, brown sugar, vanilla extract, and salt.

Melt a small pat of butter on the pan for each slice of French toast. In batches, gently press the bread slices into the egg mixture and let the mixture soak in, about 20 seconds on each side. Remove the bread slices from the egg mixture, letting the excess drip back into the bowl, and add it to the buttered pan. Cook until golden brown on each side, 2 to 3 minutes per side. Transfer to the rack and keep warm in the oven while you cook the rest of the bread.

Serve the French toast with whipped cream and a drizzle of melted chocolate.

MAKES 8 TO 10 SLICES

1 loaf Chocolate Chunk Cranberry Bread (page 29)

4 eggs

2 egg yolks

½ cup whole milk

¼ cup firmly packed brown sugar

1 teaspoon vanilla extract

¼ teaspoon salt

¼ cup cold butter

Whipped cream and melted chocolate for serving

BANANA BREAD FRENCH TOAST

We already know how popular banana bread is, but what if we turn it into French toast? It's a good choice, guys, trust me! I like to serve mine with powdered sugar and sliced bananas on top for a super banana-y breakfast!

MAKES 8 TO 10 SLICES

1 loaf Banana Bread (page 83)

3 eggs

1 egg yolk

⅓ cup whole milk

3 tablespoons firmly packed brown sugar

1 teaspoon vanilla extract

⅛ teaspoon salt

3 to 4 tablespoons butter

1 banana, sliced

Powdered sugar and pure maple syrup for serving

Preheat your oven to 200°F and set a wire rack inside of a large baking sheet. Cut the banana bread into 1-inch slices. Lay out the slices on the baking rack, and bake until the bread starts to feel lightly crisp, 8 to 10 minutes.

Heat a large skillet over medium heat. In a wide, shallow bowl, whisk together the eggs, egg yolk, milk, brown sugar, vanilla extract, and salt.

Melt a small pat of the butter in the pan before cooking each slice. Gently press the banana bread slices into the egg mixture and let the mixture soak in, about 20 seconds on each side. Remove the bread slices from the egg mixture, letting the excess drip back into the bowl, and add them to the buttered pan. Cook until golden brown on each side, 2 to 3 minutes per side. Transfer to the rack and keep warm in the oven while you cook the remaining slices.

Serve with sliced bananas, powdered sugar, and maple syrup.

BLUEBERRY FRENCH TOAST BAKE

This dish is part blueberry muffin, part bread pudding, part French toast—
so basically, it's everything. It's an easy way to serve a big breakfast,
and you can swap in other berries or chocolate chips, if you like.

To make the crumb topping, in a small bowl, using a fork, mix together the melted butter, brown sugar, flour, coarse sugar, chopped walnuts, cinnamon, and salt. The mixture should form crumbs that hold together when pressed and crumble apart easily. If the topping is too wet, add more flour, a tablespoon at a time, until you reach a crumbly consistency.

Preheat your oven to 300°F and place a wire rack in a large baking sheet.

To make the French toast, spread the bread cubes in a single layer on the rack. Bake until the bread feels crisp, about 10 minutes. Let cool.

In a large bowl, whisk together the milk, cream, brown sugar, eggs, vanilla, cinnamon, and salt until no streaks of egg yolks remain. Add the blueberries and cooled bread cubes and stir until well coated in the custard mixture. Cover and place in the fridge for 30 minutes. Meanwhile, preheat the oven to 350°F and generously butter a 2.5-quart baking dish.

Pour the custard mixture into the buttered baking dish, pressing the bread down gently to ensure that it's mostly submerged. Evenly sprinkle the crumb topping over the top. Bake until the casserole looks puffed and golden brown on top, 40 to 45 minutes. It should jiggle just slightly but should no longer be liquidy. Cool the casserole for 10 to 15 minutes before serving with powdered sugar and maple syrup!

MAKES 6 TO 8 GENEROUS SERVINGS

FOR THE CRUMB TOPPING:

¼ cup butter, melted

¼ cup firmly packed brown sugar

½ cup all-purpose flour, plus more if needed

¼ cup coarse sugar

¼ cup chopped walnuts

1 teaspoon ground cinnamon

Pinch salt

FOR THE FRENCH TOAST:

½ large loaf Basic White Bread (page 21), cut into 1-inch cubes

1 cup whole milk

¾ cup heavy cream

⅓ cup firmly packed dark brown sugar

4 eggs

1 tablespoon vanilla extract

1 teaspoon ground cinnamon

½ teaspoon salt

1 cup fresh blueberries

Butter for greasing

Powdered sugar and pure maple syrup for serving

STUFFED FRENCH TOAST

If you've never had cream cheese–stuffed French toast, today should be the day. I've topped mine with a little chocolate hazelnut spread and whipped cream, but some macerated berries and sliced bananas are a nice choice too.

MAKES 4 LARGE PIECES

FOR THE FILLING:

8 ounces cream cheese,
   at room temperature

⅓ cup sugar

1 teaspoon vanilla extract

FOR THE FRENCH TOAST:

4 slices Basic White Bread (page 21),
   each 1½ to 2 inches thick

6 eggs

⅓ cup whole milk

⅓ cup firmly packed brown sugar

½ teaspoon ground cinnamon

¼ teaspoon salt

2 to 3 tablespoons cold butter

¼ cup chocolate-hazelnut spread

½ cup whipped cream

To make the filling, in a large bowl, whisk together the cream cheese, sugar, and vanilla extract until smooth and well blended. Set aside.

To make the French toast, preheat the oven to the lowest setting (that's 170°F for me), if desired. Put a wire rack inside a rimmed baking sheet and set aside.

Using a sharp knife, cut along the side of each slice (the side with crust) to create a large pocket in each slice of bread. The pocket should be large enough to stuff with filling without breaking through the other side of the bread. Then, gently spoon a generous amount of the cream cheese filling into each pocket. You should be able to divide all the filling among all 4 slices.

Heat a large skillet over medium heat. Meanwhile, in a wide, shallow bowl, whisk together the eggs, milk, brown sugar, cinnamon, and salt.

Melt 1 tablespoon butter in the skillet. Dip a stuffed piece of bread into the egg mixture and let the mixture soak in, about 30 seconds on each side. Remove the bread from the egg mixture, letting the excess drip back into the bowl, and add it to the buttered pan. Cook until golden brown, 3 to 4 minutes per side. Transfer to the rack and keep warm in the oven while you cook the rest of the pieces. ·

Top each piece with the toppings of your choice—in my case that's a good swoop of chocolate-hazelnut spread and a dollop of whipped cream. Enjoy!

FRENCH TOAST DIPPERS

I've always loved French toast dippers because they are so easy to eat, and less messy than a plateful of maple syrup. Making them is super simple, and I'm opting for Brioche bread here to make a really rich, flavorful dipper.

Warm a large skillet over medium heat and preheat your oven to the lowest setting (mine is 170°F). Put a wire rack inside a rimmed baking sheet and set aside.

Heat a large skillet over medium heat. Slice your brioche into 1-inch slices, and then slice each piece into 4 thick sticks.

In a wide, shallow bowl or dish, whisk together the eggs, cream, vanilla extract, brown sugar, and salt. Melt 1 tablespoon of butter onto your pan for each batch of French Toast Dippers that you cook. Dip the bread into the mixture, coating all sides. Remove the bread sticks from the egg mixture, letting the excess drip back into the bowl, and add them to the buttered pan. Cook until all sides are golden brown, 1 to 2 minutes on each of 4 sides. Transfer to the rack and keep warm in the oven while you cook the rest of the bread pieces.

Serve with maple syrup for dipping.

MAKES ABOUT 30 DIPPERS

1 loaf Brioche (page 23)

4 eggs

½ cup heavy cream

1 teaspoon vanilla extract

3 tablespoons firmly packed brown sugar

⅛ teaspoon salt

2 to 3 tablespoons butter

Pure maple syrup for serving

SAVORY FRENCH TOAST
WITH HOLLANDAISE

This decadent, savory French toast is topped with a lemony hollandaise and a crispy fried egg. It gives croque madame vibes, and it's a welcome twist on a classic breakfast dish. There are a lot of steps to get through here, but it comes together as an indulgent, truly delicious breakfast. Trust me, it's worth it!

MAKES 2 SERVINGS

4 slices Basic White Bread (page 21), each ¾- to 1-inch thick

5 eggs

3 tablespoons whole milk

3 tablespoons finely grated Parmesan cheese, plus more for sprinkling

1 teaspoon salt

1 teaspoon freshly ground black pepper

½ teaspoon paprika

½ teaspoon chili powder

3 to 4 tablespoons butter

Warm a large skillet over medium heat and preheat your oven to the lowest setting (mine is 170°F). Put a wire rack inside a rimmed baking sheet and set aside.

In a large bowl, or a wide dish with tall edges, beat together 3 of the eggs, the milk, Parmesan cheese, salt, pepper, paprika, and chili powder until well blended.

Melt 1 tablespoon butter in the heated pan. Dip a bread slice into the egg mixture, coating both sides for about 20 seconds per side, and then place it in your pan. Cook until golden brown on both sides, 2 to 3 minutes per side. Transfer the cooked slices to the rack and put in the oven to stay warm. Continue to soak and cook the remaining slices.

CONTINUED ON NEXT PAGE

SAVORY FRENCH TOAST
WITH HOLLANDAISE (CONTINUED)

FOR THE HOLLANDAISE:

2 egg yolks

1 tablespoon fresh lemon juice

½ teaspoon salt

¼ teaspoon cayenne pepper
(or freshly ground black pepper
for less spice)

½ cup butter, melted

2 tablespoons canola oil

For the hollandaise, place a heatproof bowl over (not touching) a saucepan of just simmering water. In the bowl, whisk together the egg yolks, lemon juice, salt, and cayenne pepper, whisking constantly until the mixture becomes pale and a little thickened, 5 to 8 minutes. While continuing to whisk, very slowly mix in the melted butter; it should take you a few minutes to get all the butter incorporated. If the butter is added too fast, the mixture might break. Turn off the heat and let the hollandaise sit over the water, whisking occasionally, to keep it warm.

Place the same skillet you used for the French toast over medium-high heat and add the canola oil. Once the pan is hot, crack in the remaining 2 eggs and cook to your desired doneness—I prefer over-medium, which should take about 1 to 2 minutes per side.

Now it's time to assemble! Remove the French toast from the oven and place one piece of French toast on each of 2 serving plates. Top that with a little bit of hollandaise, and another piece of French toast. Then, add a fried egg on top of each stack, more hollandaise, and a little sprinkle of Parmesan cheese.

Serve right away.

BREAKFAST TARTS

These are amped up, super yummy versions of the toaster breakfast pastries of our childhood. I've got three filling and frosting options for you guys, and they are all insanely good. Pick your favorite option among the three flavors.

Line a large baking sheet with parchment paper and set aside. Using a rolling pin, roll out the pie crust on a floured work surface into a large rectangle about ⅛-inch thick. Cut the dough into twelve 2½-inch squares (I use a square pastry cutter for this). Arrange 6 of the squares on the prepared baking sheet, spacing them evenly. Brush the edges of each square with the beaten egg.

To make berry tarts, fill each square with a dollop of your jam. Top with another pie crust square and press all around the edges to seal. Using a fork, crimp the edges all around. Chill the tarts in the fridge for 20 minutes. Meanwhile, preheat your oven to 375°F. Brush the tart tops with more of the beaten egg and bake until golden brown all over, 16 to 18 minutes. Let cool.

In a small bowl, whisk together the powdered sugar, freeze-dried strawberries, salt, and 2 tablespoons water to make an icing. Add more water if needed to reach the right consistency.

After the tarts have cooled for 10 minutes, spread the icing over the top, and top with sprinkles, if you like! Serve warm or at room temperature.

To make brown sugar–cinnamon tarts, in a small bowl, stir together the ½ cup brown sugar, 1 teaspoon of the cinnamon, the ginger, nutmeg, and flour.

MAKES 6 TARTS

1 batch Classic Pie Crust (page 214), unbaked

Flour for rolling

1 egg, lightly beaten

FOR BERRY TARTS:

½ cup blackberry jam

1 cup powdered sugar

2 tablespoons powdered freeze-dried strawberries

⅛ teaspoon salt

2 to 3 tablespoons water

2 tablespoons sprinkles (optional)

FOR BROWN SUGAR–CINNAMON TARTS:

½ cup plus 2 tablespoons firmly packed brown sugar

1½ teaspoons ground cinnamon

1 teaspoon ground ginger

½ teaspoon ground nutmeg

1 tablespoon all-purpose flour

1 cup powdered sugar

⅛ teaspoon salt

2 to 3 tablespoons water

2 tablespoons sprinkles (optional)

CONTINUED ON NEXT PAGE

BREAKFAST TARTS (CONTINUED)

Spoon small piles of the mixture in the center of each pie crust square. Top with another square of crust and press down on the edges to seal. Using a fork, crimp the edges all around. Chill the tarts in the fridge for 20 minutes. Meanwhile, preheat your oven to 375°F. Brush the tops with more beaten egg, and bake until golden brown all over, 16 to 18 minutes. Let cool.

In a small bowl, whisk together the powdered sugar, remaining 2 tablespoons brown sugar, remaining ½ teaspoon cinnamon, the salt, and 2 tablespoons water to make an icing. Add more water if needed to reach the right consistency.

After the tarts have cooled for 10 minutes, spread the icing over the top, and top with sprinkles, if you like! Serve warm or at room temperature.

To make chocolate tarts, in a small bowl, stir together the chocolate-hazelnut spread, espresso powder, and ⅛ teaspoon of the salt until blended. Spoon a dollop of the mixture in the center of each pie crust square. Top with another pie crust square and press all around the edges to seal. Using a fork, crimp the edges all around. Chill the tarts in the fridge for 20 minutes. Meanwhile, preheat your oven to 375°F. Brush the tart tops with more of the beaten egg and bake until golden brown all over, 16 to 18 minutes. Let cool.

In a small bowl, whisk together the powdered sugar, cocoa powder, remaining ⅛ teaspoon salt, and 2 tablespoons water to make an icing. Add more water if needed to reach the right consistency.

After the tarts have cooled for 10 minutes, spread the icing over the top, and top with sprinkles, if you like!

FOR CHOCOLATE TARTS:

½ cup chocolate-hazelnut spread

⅛ teaspoon instant espresso powder

¼ teaspoon salt

1 cup powdered sugar

2 tablespoons Dutch process
   cocoa powder

2 to 3 tablespoons water

2 tablespoons sprinkles (optional)

BREAKFAST SANDWICHES

To me the reason that breakfast sandwiches are so good is because they are incredibly flexible. You can turn any breakfast foods that you like into breakfast sandwiches, like the Maple Bacon Waffle Sandwich, and you can fill them with whatever you have on hand. I love the Breakfast Grilled Cheese for a lazy Sunday brunch, and the Bacon & Tomato Biscuit Sliders are a perfect on-the-go choice. Whatever you feel like eating, a breakfast sandwich is the answer!

HAM & JAM SLIDERS

These are super simple, but super yummy. You can use any jam you prefer, but I like a spicy berry jam for these sliders to give them a little kick!

Preheat your oven to 350°F and lightly grease a 9-by-13-inch baking pan.

Slice the slider buns in half crosswise and layer each bun with a couple of folded slices of ham. Spread a dollop of the spicy jam on the top half of the slider bun and place it on top of the ham.

Arrange the sliders into the prepared baking pan and bake until warmed through and the jam is sticky and yummy, about 10 minutes. Serve warm.

MAKES 12 SLIDERS

1 batch Everything Bagel Slider Buns (page 39)

1 pound thickly sliced ham

¼ cup spicy berry jam

MAPLE BACON WAFFLE SANDWICHES

This sandwich is a lazy weekend, hangover-friendly, completely cozy meal.
The maple bacon creates a sweet addition to a fried egg with a runny yolk
that drips into the pockets of a waffle, along with some sharp cheddar.
I love all the sandwiches in this book, but this one is my ideal option!

MAKES 4 SANDWICHES

1 batch Basic Waffles (page 117)

½ pound sliced bacon

¼ cup pure maple syrup

3 tablespoons firmly packed
   brown sugar

½ teaspoon freshly ground
   black pepper

½ teaspoon salt

Canola oil

4 eggs

½ cup shredded cheddar cheese

Cook the waffles according to the recipe instructions
and set aside; you'll need 8 waffles for this dish.

Preheat your oven to 400°F and line a large baking
sheet with multiple layers of foil. Arrange the bacon
strips in a single layer on the prepared pan. In a
small bowl, stir together the maple syrup, brown
sugar, pepper, and salt until combined. Generously
brush the syrup mixture onto each strip of bacon.
Bake for 15 minutes.

Remove the bacon from the oven and flip all the
bacon strips over. Brush the other sides with more
glaze, and return to the oven until they're brown and
cooked through, about 10 more minutes. Immediately
transfer the bacon to a plate to rest.

In a skillet coated with a thin layer of canola oil, fry
4 eggs until cooked to your liking—I like them over-
medium with a runny yolk.

To assemble, pop the waffles into a toaster to rewarm
them. Divide the warm waffles among 4 serving plates.
Top 4 waffles with a fried egg, a sprinkle of cheese,
and 2 slices of the maple-glazed bacon. Cover each
with a second waffle and serve right away. Enjoy!

BACON & EGG BISCUIT SANDWICHES

A flaky biscuit isn't always the most stable vehicle for a sandwich, so it's a great time to use an omelet as a sandwich filling. All of the bacon and cheese is cooked right into the eggs, making a low-mess breakfast sandwich.

In a skillet, warm the vegetable oil over medium heat. Meanwhile, in a small bowl, whisk together the eggs, salt, pepper, chopped bacon, and cheddar cheese until well mixed. Pour the egg mixture into the hot pan and cook, stirring, until the eggs start to set. Stop stirring and cook until the eggs are fully set on the bottom, covering the bottom of the pan, and the eggs are mostly cooked on top. Use a flexible spatula to flip half of the omelet onto the other half. Cook for another 1 to 2 minutes, or until the eggs are fully cooked.

Remove the omelet from the pan and cut the omelet into 4 even sections. Slice your biscuits in half crosswise. Put the biscuit bottoms on serving plates and top with the warm omelet pieces. Cover with the biscuit tops and enjoy!

MAKES 4 SANDWICHES

1 tablespoon vegetable oil

3 eggs

1 teaspoon salt

½ teaspoon freshly ground black pepper

3 strips cooked bacon, chopped

¼ cup shredded sharp cheddar cheese

4 Cream Biscuits (page 70)

SAUSAGE & ONION BREAKFAST SANDWICHES

Caramelized onions make this breakfast sandwich really flavorful, and it's got tons of cheese on top, too. I love a good breakfast sandwich, and this one is made with a crispy fried egg on top for the ultimate breakfast experience.

MAKES 4 SANDWICHES

2 tablespoons olive oil

1 yellow onion

½ teaspoon salt

½ teaspoon freshly ground black pepper

4 sausage patties

4 large eggs

4 English Muffins (page 53)

¼ cup shredded cheddar cheese

In a large skillet, warm the olive oil over medium heat. Slice the onion pole to pole into long slivers and add to the skillet along with the salt and pepper. Cook, stirring frequently, until the onions become translucent, 3 to 4 minutes. Reduce the heat to medium-low and cook the onions, stirring frequently, until they reach a deep golden-brown color, 15 to 20 minutes. Remove the onions from the pan and wipe it out with a paper towel.

Warm the same skillet over medium-high heat and cook the sausage patties until both sides are deeply browned and each patty is cooked through, 3 to 4 minutes per side. Transfer the sausage patties to a plate lined with paper towels to drain.

Leave the fat in the skillet, add the eggs, and cook over medium-high heat until crispy and fried, 1 to 2 minutes per side.

Slice the English muffins in half crosswise and toast until golden. Divide the English muffin bottoms among 4 serving plates. Top each with a layer of onions, a sausage patty, a crispy fried egg, and a tablespoon of the cheddar cheese. Cover with the English muffin tops. Serve with lots of napkins!

BACON & TOMATO BISCUIT SLIDERS

Savory biscuits are the perfect vehicle for small slider sandwiches with a generous schmear of cream cheese. These are one of my favorite sandwiches in the whole book, and they pack some big flavor.

Slice your biscuits in half crosswise and set aside. Cut the cherry tomatoes in half and set those aside as well.

In a large skillet over medium heat, cook the turkey bacon until browned on both sides, about 5 minutes per side. Cut each slice of bacon in half.

To assemble the sliders, spread a few tablespoons of cream cheese on each biscuit bottom, and sprinkle with salt and pepper. Top each with 4 to 5 tomato halves and 2 turkey bacon pieces. Cover with the biscuit tops and serve right away.

MAKES 6 SLIDERS

1 batch Savory Biscuits (page 69)

1 cup cherry tomatoes

6 slices turkey bacon

½ cup cream cheese, softened

1 teaspoon salt

½ teaspoon freshly ground black pepper

AVOCADO & GREEN CHILE BREAKFAST SANDWICHES

This is one of the best breakfast sandwiches you can make at home. The green chiles give a little spice, and combined with the tomato and avocado it's completely perfect. You won't even miss the cheese on this one!

MAKES 4 SANDWICHES

4 English Muffins (page 53)

2 tablespoons butter

5 eggs

3 tablespoons whole milk

1¼ teaspoons salt

½ teaspoon freshly ground black pepper

1 to 2 tablespoons diced green chiles

4 thin slices tomato

½ large avocado, thinly sliced

Slice your English muffins in half crosswise and toast them in a toaster until golden brown.

Warm a skillet over medium-low heat and add the butter. In a bowl, beat together the eggs, milk, 1 teaspoon of the salt, and the pepper until well combined. When the butter is melted, pour the eggs into the skillet and cook, stirring frequently. Once the eggs begin to set, add the green chiles to your taste. Cook the egg mixture until just set, or until cooked to your liking.

To assemble, divide the English muffin bottoms among 4 serving plates. Top each with a slice of tomato and lightly sprinkle with salt. Top each with the scrambled egg mixture, dividing evenly, and a few slices of avocado. Cover with the English muffin tops and serve right away.

BREAKFAST GRILLED CHEESE

If you didn't know, there's literally no reason you can't have a grilled cheese for breakfast! This version has an egg fried right into the bread, and it's so simple but so delicious. I'd call this one the hangover cure for sure!

Heat a large skillet over medium heat. Spread a thin layer of butter on one side of 2 slices of the bread, and both sides of the other 2 slices of bread. Using a 2-inch round cutter, cut holes out of the centers of the two slices of double-buttered bread.

Place the cutout pieces of bread into your skillet and immediately crack an egg into the hole of each slice of bread. (You can toast the "holes" on the side of the pan for a little snack.) Cook until the bread is toasted on the bottom and the egg is cooked enough through to allow you to flip it, 1 to 2 minutes. Flip both pieces. Then, top each portion with generous piles of cheddar and Monterey Jack cheese, and 2 slices of bacon per sandwich. Top with the remaining slices of bread, buttered side out. Cook until golden brown on the bottom side, 2 to 3 minutes, and then flip the sandwich again. Cook until the other side is golden brown, the egg is cooked through, and the cheese has melted, 3 to 4 more minutes. Serve warm.

MAKES 2 SANDWICHES

4 tablespoons butter, softened

4 slices Basic White Bread (page 21)

2 eggs

½ cup shredded sharp cheddar cheese

½ cup shredded Monterey Jack cheese

4 slices bacon, cooked until crisp

BISCUITS WITH BACON GRAVY

You can make this recipe with breakfast sausage instead of bacon,
but bacon is an interesting and super yummy twist on the
classic biscuits and gravy. These open-faced "sandwiches"
use the cream biscuits as their base, and it's the perfect combo.

MAKES 3 TO 4 SERVINGS

1 pound sliced bacon

4 tablespoons all-purpose flour

2 cups whole milk

2 to 3 teaspoons salt

1 to 2 teaspoons freshly ground
   black pepper

3 to 4 eggs (optional)

6 Cream Biscuits (page 70)

In a large skillet over medium-high heat, fry the
bacon in batches until browned and crisp. You want
the bacon to be on the well-done side for this dish so
that it doesn't get soggy when you add it to the gravy.
Let the cooked bacon drain and cool on a plate lined
with paper towels.

You want to have about 5 tablespoons of bacon grease
left in the pan, so pour out any excess (it doesn't need
to be exact). Place the skillet over medium heat and
whisk in the flour until it forms a thick paste. Let the
flour paste cook for 2 to 3 minutes to cook the flour
flavor out a bit. Then, slowly stream in the milk while
you continue to whisk until all the milk has been
added. Stir in 2 teaspoons salt and 1 teaspoon black
pepper, and cook the gravy until it becomes thick,
2 to 3 minutes. Taste for seasoning and add more salt
and pepper if needed.

Meanwhile, crumble the bacon into small pieces. Once
the gravy has thickened, add the bacon to the gravy
and stir to mix.

To serve, slice the biscuits in half crosswise and
divide among serving plates. Top with a generous
amount of the bacon gravy. Serve warm.

EGG-BASED BREAKFASTS

I'm a fan of eggs for dinner pretty much anytime. This section is filled with all my favorite egg dishes, including the classics like Eggs Benedict (with homemade English Muffins, of course!) all the way to a Breakfast Panzanella that I can't stop making. Eggs can be tricky at high altitude because they often have different cooking times than at sea-level. While boiled eggs can take longer to cook because it takes longer for water to boil here, stovetop cooked eggs can often cook quicker because of the faster liquid evaporation at higher altitudes.

CLASSIC EGGS BENEDICT

Making eggs Benedict on homemade English muffins is such a treat.
I love a lemony hollandaise sauce on top, and classic sliced ham on
the muffins, but you can use any breakfast meat you want here.
It's also super yummy topped with sliced avocado!

MAKES 2 SERVINGS

2 English Muffins (page 53)

4 slices deli-style ham

Hollandaise (page 168)

4 eggs

1 green onion, thinly sliced

Slice the English muffins in half crosswise and toast them in a toaster until golden brown. Arrange the English muffin bottoms on serving plates, cut sides up. In a saucepan, bring 3 inches of water to a gentle simmer over medium heat.

Meanwhile, heat a skillet over medium heat and quickly fry the ham slices. They should just start to sizzle and get some color, but mostly you just want to warm them through. Lay the sliced ham on top of each English muffin half, folding them if needed.

Prepare the hollandaise according to the recipe and keep warm, whisking occasionally.

One at a time, crack the eggs into small bowls to make sure you don't break the yolks, and then gently ease 2 of the eggs into the simmering water. Using a large spoon, immediately give the water a gentle stir to help hold the shape of the egg. Let the eggs simmer in the water until they are white on the outside and starting to set, 3 to 4 minutes. Using a slotted spoon, gently remove each egg from the simmering water, shaking slightly to remove any excess water, and set aside on a plate. Repeat to cook the remaining eggs.

Place 1 egg on each English muffin half on top of the ham. Top with a generous spoonful of hollandaise and a sprinkle of the green onions. Serve right away.

BAGEL STRATA

A strata is kind of like a cross between a quiche and bread pudding. You can use any type of bread you like, including Basic White Bread (page 21), Gruyère-Cheddar Bread (page 41), or even English Muffins (page 53). The fillings are flexible as well, so go with whatever veggies and cheese you have on hand!

MAKES 6 TO 8 SERVINGS

Butter, for greasing

5 Bagels (page 35), or about 5 thick slices of your choice of bread (see note)

3 tablespoons olive oil

1 pint white mushrooms, thickly sliced

1 small yellow onion, chopped

4 cloves garlic, minced

1 tablespoon salt

2 teaspoons freshly ground black pepper

8 eggs

½ cup whole milk

1 cup shredded cheddar cheese

Preheat your oven to 350°F. Generously grease a 10-inch cast-iron skillet or a 2-quart baking dish with butter and set aside.

Cut your bagels into cubes about 1-inch in size and arrange them in a single layer on a large baking sheet. Bake until the bagel cubes are starting to get crisp and dried out, 10 to 12 minutes. Set aside.

Warm a skillet over medium heat and add the olive oil. When the oil is hot, add the mushrooms and onion and cook, stirring occasionally, for 8 to 10 minutes—the mushrooms should lose their moisture, and the onions should be soft. Stir in the minced garlic, 1 teaspoon of the salt, and 1 teaspoon of the pepper, and cook the mixture until the vegetables are soft, another 1 to 2 minutes. Remove from the heat.

In a large bowl, whisk together the eggs, milk, remaining 2 teaspoons salt and 1 teaspoon black pepper until well blended. Stir in the cheese, cooked mushroom and onion mixture, and toasted bagel cubes. Push the bagels down into the egg mixture to make sure they are fully submerged and cover with plastic wrap. Let the mixture stand at room temperature for 20 minutes.

Pour the entire mixture into your prepared skillet or baking dish and bake until the top is golden brown and the middle has set, 45 to 50 minutes. Serve hot.

BREAKFAST PANZANELLA

I like to think of Panzanella as a bread salad, and who doesn't want to
eat bread and call it a salad? This one is topped with poached eggs
for a breakfast twist, and it makes a hearty, comforting meal!

MAKES 4 SERVINGS

FOR THE SALAD:

¾ loaf Basic White Bread (page 21)

3 large heirloom tomatoes, cut into
large, bite-size chunks

2 tablespoons olive oil

1 teaspoon salt

FOR THE DRESSING:

¼ cup olive oil

3 tablespoons fresh lemon juice
(from 1 lemon)

1 teaspoon salt

½ teaspoon freshly ground
black pepper

½ teaspoon dried basil

4 eggs

1 avocado, cut into small chunks

¼ cup chopped fresh parsley

To make the salad, preheat your oven to 200°F. Using
your hands, tear the bread into large chunks and
spread evenly on a large baking sheet. Bake until
dried and crisp, about 15 minutes.

Increase the oven temperature to 450°F. Toss the
tomatoes with the bread (still on the baking sheet),
2 tablespoons olive oil, and 1 teaspoon salt. Spread
the bread-tomato mixture into an even layer. Bake
until the bread starts to toast and the tomatoes are
sizzling, 10 to 12 minutes.

To make the dressing, in a small bowl, whisk together
the oil, lemon juice, salt, pepper, and dried basil until
well blended.

To poach the eggs, fill a deep-sided skillet or a
shallow pot with 2 to 3 inches of water and bring it
to a gentle simmer over medium heat. Crack an egg
into a small bowl to make sure you don't break the
yolk and gently ease it into the simmering water.
Using a large spoon, immediately give the water a
gentle stir to help hold the shape of the egg. Let the
egg simmer until the white on the outside is starting
to set, 3 to 4 minutes. Using a slotted spoon, gently
transfer the egg to a plate lined with paper towels.
Repeat to poach the remaining eggs.

Put generous piles of the bread and tomato mixture
onto serving plates. Top each with a poached egg, a
few chunks of avocado, a sprinkle of parsley, and
a generous drizzle of the dressing. Serve right away.

FRIED RICE & EGGS

This is what my dad cooked us for breakfast every weekend when I was growing up, and it's a super satisfying dish. You can top yours with whatever you'd like, and leftover rice is a perfect substitute for cooking your own in the morning. This is a nostalgic dish for me, and I hope you love it just as much!

Place the rice in a mesh sieve and rinse under running cold water, agitating it with your hands, for several minutes, until the water runs fairly clear. Pour the rice into a saucepan and add the 1¾ cups water and the salt. Bring the rice to a boil, uncovered, over medium-high heat and then reduce the heat to low and cover. Cook, without opening the lid, until the rice is tender and the liquid has cooked out, 18 to 20 minutes. Place a clean dishtowel under the lid of your pot, cover with the lid, and let the rice stand off the heat for another 5 minutes.

Fluff the rice with a fork. In a large skillet over medium-high heat, warm 2 tablespoons of the oil. Add the rice and chili powder and cook, stirring occasionally, until the rice is warmed through and lightly crispy. Divide the rice among serving plates and keep warm while you fry the eggs.

Return the pan to medium-high heat and add the remaining 2 tablespoons oil. Crack the eggs into the pan and cook for 1 to 2 minutes on each side for over-easy eggs, or until done to your liking. Place 2 eggs on top of each serving of rice. Sprinkle with soy sauce and green onions to taste. Enjoy!

MAKES 2 SERVINGS

1 cup long-grain white rice

1¾ cups water

1 teaspoon salt

4 tablespoons vegetable oil

1 teaspoon chili powder

4 eggs

2 to 4 tablespoons soy sauce

2 to 3 green onions, thinly sliced

HAM & CHEDDAR QUICHE

This quiche has simple flavors, but the cheese cracker crust brings it
to a whole new level. I love baking a quiche on a Sunday
afternoon and enjoying it for breakfast all week long before work!

MAKES 8 SERVINGS

1 Cheese Cracker Crust (page 215),
  prepared in an 8-inch pie plate

2 tablespoons olive oil

2 cups fresh spinach

6 eggs

½ cup whole milk

¼ cup sour cream

1 cup shredded cheddar cheese

1 teaspoon salt

1 teaspoon freshly ground
  black pepper

1½ cups chopped ham
  (from thick slices)

¼ cup thinly sliced green onions

Preheat your oven to 350°F. Heat a large skillet over
medium heat and add the olive oil and spinach. Cook,
stirring frequently, until the spinach is wilted, about
5 minutes. Set it aside to cool.

In a large bowl, whisk together the eggs, milk, and
sour cream until well blended. Stir in the cheese,
salt, pepper, ham, green onions, and cooled spinach.
Pour the entire mixture into your prepared pie crust.
Bake the quiche until the top is golden brown and
puffed and the middle is set, 35 to 40 minutes.

Let cool for 10 minutes before slicing and serving.

BREAKFAST PIZZA

Pizza is an every-meal dish, and even though I've been known
to eat a slice of cold pepperoni for breakfast, a full-on breakfast pizza
is the way to go! You can use sausage like I did, or
crumbled bacon—even small chunks of ham would be perfect here!

Place a large baking sheet in your oven on the middle
rack and preheat the oven to 450°F.

In a large skillet over medium-high heat, cook the
sausage until it is fully browned and crumbled.

When the oven is hot, remove the heated pan and
drizzle it with 2 tablespoons of the olive oil. Gently
stretch the pizza dough with your hands into a very
large rectangle that fits into your baking sheet pan
and carefully place it on the pan (remember, it's hot!).
Drizzle the dough with the remaining 1 tablespoon
olive oil. Then, evenly sprinkle on most of the
mozzarella and Parmesan cheeses, reserving a little
for the top. Sprinkle with the sliced cherry tomatoes
and the cooked turkey sausage. Finally, sprinkle with
the reserved cheese. Bake the pizza for 10 minutes,
and then remove it from the oven.

Crack your eggs directly onto the pizza, spacing them
over the whole pizza. Sprinkle the salt and pepper on
top. Put the pizza back until the crust is golden brown
and the eggs have cooked but still have runny yolks,
about 5 more minutes.

Slice and serve hot!

MAKES 1 LARGE PIZZA

1 pound bulk turkey sausage

3 tablespoons olive oil

1 batch Simple Pizza Dough
(page 215)

2 cups shredded mozzarella cheese

½ cup freshly grated Parmesan
cheese

1 cup cherry tomatoes, sliced in half

5 eggs

1 teaspoon salt

½ teaspoon freshly ground
black pepper

CINNAMON BREAD PUDDING

If bread pudding makes you think of dessert, you've never had a breakfast one! It's so much like French toast that it makes the perfect breakfast. This version is made with Cinnamon Swirl Bread, and it's topped with a super easy brown sugar sauce!

MAKES 6 SERVINGS

FOR THE BREAD PUDDING:

1 loaf Cinnamon Swirl Bread (page 33), cut into cubes

1 cups whole milk

¾ cup heavy cream

⅓ cup firmly packed brown sugar

3 eggs

1 tablespoon vanilla extract

¼ teaspoon salt

¼ teaspoon ground nutmeg

¼ teaspoon ground cloves

¼ teaspoon ground cinnamon

Cooking spray

FOR THE SAUCE:

1 cup heavy cream

½ cup firmly packed brown sugar

¼ teaspoon salt

2 teaspoons vanilla extract

To make the bread pudding, preheat your oven to 350°F. Arrange the bread cubes evenly on a large sheet pan and bake until the bread is starting to toast and dry out, 10 to 12 minutes. Let the bread cool.

In a large bowl, whisk together the milk, cream, brown sugar, eggs, vanilla extract, salt, nutmeg, cloves, and cinnamon until well blended and smooth. Add the toasted bread cubes, pressing them down gently to make sure that all the bread gets coated in the custard mixture. Cover with plastic wrap and let the mixture stand at room temperature for 20 minutes.

Meanwhile, generously grease an 8-inch round or square cake pan with cooking spray. Pour the entire mixture into the pan, spreading it evenly and gently pressing the bread down to submerge it in the egg mixture if needed. Bake until the mixture is lightly golden on top and the middle is set, 42 to 45 minutes.

To make the sauce, in a small saucepan, stir together the cream, brown sugar, salt, and vanilla extract. Heat over medium-high heat until boiling, and then whisk frequently while boiling the mixture for 10 minutes. The sauce will be thick and glossy. Pour sauce over the warm bread pudding and serve!

SAUSAGE & POTATO BREAKFAST CASSEROLE

Breakfast casserole is the easiest way to make a morning meal for a crowd. We're kind of just putting together a bunch of yummy pieces of a classic breakfast and baking it all as one. I like to top mine with something crunchy, like crumbled butter crackers or crushed cornflakes!

Preheat your oven to 350°F and grease a 9-by-13-inch baking dish with cooking spray. Heat a skillet over medium-high heat, and brown the turkey sausage, breaking it into crumbles as you cook. Drain and set aside.

In a very large bowl, whisk together the eggs, sour cream, milk, salt, pepper, onion powder, garlic powder, and dill until well combined. Then, stir in the frozen hash browns, cheddar cheese, and cooked sausage until everything is well combined. Pour the mixture into your prepared pan and spread evenly. Sprinkle the crushed crackers all over the top. Bake until the top is golden brown and the middle is set, 55 to 60 minutes.

Let cool for 10 minutes before serving.

MAKES ABOUT 12 SERVINGS

Cooking spray

1 pound bulk turkey sausage

8 eggs

½ cup sour cream

¼ cup whole milk

1 tablespoon salt

1 teaspoon freshly ground black pepper

1 teaspoon onion powder

½ teaspoon garlic powder

½ teaspoon dried dill

One 30-ounce bag frozen hash browns

2 cups shredded cheddar cheese

1 sleeve prepared butter crackers, crumbled

BROCCOLI GRUYÈRE QUICHE

This is a classic quiche with a savory cheese crust that pulls everything together. It comes together quickly, and it packs big flavors that I love! It's the perfect quiche to serve to a crowd.

MAKES ONE 9-INCH QUICHE

1 Savory Pie Crust (page 215)

2 tablespoons canola oil

1 head fresh broccoli, stem removed, chopped into small pieces

6 eggs

½ cup whole milk

1 cup shredded Gruyère cheese

1 teaspoon dried dill

½ teaspoon salt

Prepare the pie crust and partially bake it according to the instructions on page 214.

In a large skillet, warm the oil over medium heat. Add the broccoli pieces and saute until it's bright green and just starting to become tender, 3 to 5 minutes.

In a large bowl, whisk together the eggs, milk, Gruyère cheese, dill, and salt until well blended. Pour the mixture into your prepared pie crust, and bake until the quiche is puffed and set, 40 to 45 minutes.

Let cool for 15 minutes before slicing and serving.

STEAK & EGG TACOS

Breakfast tacos are the perfect vehicle for every savory breakfast item you love. These are wonderful with soft scrambled eggs, like I've done here, but they're also great with an over-medium fried egg. You can swap out the steak for bacon or sausage as well, but the steak and eggs combo is seriously delicious.

In a food processor or a blender, combine the lime juice, soy sauce, 2 tablespoons of the olive oil, the onion, garlic, jalapeño, and cilantro. Process until well blended; the mixture should be slightly thick. Pour half of the mixture into a large zip-top plastic bag or wide baking dish that will fit the flank steak. Add the steak and then pour the remaining mixture on top. Spread the mixture around to coat the steak, seal or cover, and then let the steak marinate for 30 minutes.

Warm a large skillet over high heat and add the remaining 1 tablespoon olive oil. When hot, add the marinated steak—it's ok to leave some of the marinade on the steak; just give it a light shake and put it in the pan. Cook until seared on both sides and cooked to your liking, 2 to 3 minutes per side for medium doneness. Remove the steak from the pan, cover with foil, and let rest for 10 minutes before slicing.

While the steak rests, scramble the eggs: Wipe out the pan with a paper towel and place over medium-low heat. Add the butter to the skillet. When the butter is melted, pour the beaten eggs into the skillet and cook, stirring constantly, until soft scrambled, 2 to 3 minutes. Remove from the heat.

Cut the steak against the grain into thin slices. On each tortilla, layer a scoop of the scrambled eggs, a couple slices of steak, and toppings of your choice. Serve right away.

MAKES 6 TO 8 TACOS

¼ cup fresh lime juice

¼ cup soy sauce

3 tablespoons olive oil

½ onion, cut into chunks

4 cloves garlic, crushed and peeled

½ large jalapeño chile, cut into chunks, seeds retained

1 bunch fresh cilantro

1 flank steak, ¾ to 1 pound

2 tablespoons butter

4 eggs, well beaten

1 batch Flour Tortillas (page 47), cooked as small tortillas

Toppings of your choice: shredded cheddar cheese, hot sauce, avocado slices, salsa, etc.

BREAKFAST BURRITOS

Breakfast burritos are the perfect way to use your homemade tortillas, and they are super customizable. Use any cheese, any meat, and any green chile you prefer, and make this spicy jalapeño cream sauce for dipping! The sauce is also good on other types of burritos and tacos.

MAKES 5 TO 6 BURRITOS

FOR THE BURRITOS:

½ pound bulk breakfast sausage

1 large russet potato

Salt and freshly ground black pepper

1 cup prepared Southwestern-style pork green chili

4 to 6 eggs

2 tablespoons butter

½ cup shredded cheddar cheese

1 batch Flour Tortillas (page 47), cooked as large tortillas

FOR THE JALAPEÑO CREAM SAUCE (OPTIONAL):

½ cup sour cream

1 large jalapeño chile, seeds removed, chopped

2 tablespoons fresh lime juice

2 green onions, trimmed and roughly chopped

2 cloves garlic

¾ teaspoon salt

¼ teaspoon freshly ground black pepper

To make the burritos, in a large skillet, cook the breakfast sausage until browned, and then remove and drain it on a plate lined with paper towels. Peel the potato and chop it into small, bite-sized chunks. Cook the potatoes in the same skillet over medium heat, tossing occasionally, until soft and browned, 5 to 10 minutes. Season to taste with salt and pepper. Add the sausage back to the pan along with the Southwestern-style pork green chili and stir to mix. Set the mixture over very low heat to keep warm.

In a bowl, whisk together the eggs with a pinch of salt and pepper. In another skillet, melt the butter over medium heat. Pour in the eggs and cook, stirring constantly, until scrambled and fully cooked.

To assemble the burritos, fill each tortilla with a scoop of eggs; top that with a generous sprinkle of cheese; and then add a scoop of the warm sausage, potato, and green chili mixture. Roll the burritos tightly and place on serving plates.

To make the sauce, if desired, combine the sour cream, jalapeno, lime juice, green onions, garlic, salt, and pepper in a small food processor and blend together until smooth. (You can also use a blender, or an immersion blender if you don't have a small processor.) Set small bowls of the sauce on serving plates for dipping.

BASIC RECIPES

CLASSIC PIE CRUST

I've made so many different pie crust recipes over the years, I couldn't possibly count them. There are so many ways to make pie crust, but I find that adding an egg to the mixture helps keep the dough tender, while the folding process helps to keep it flaky. Use this for the Breakfast Tarts (page 169) or any type of breakfast pie you like.

MAKES 1 LARGE PIE CRUST

1¾ cups all-purpose flour, plus more for rolling

3 tablespoons sugar

½ teaspoon salt

¾ cup very cold butter

1 egg

¼ cup cold water

1 teaspoon vanilla extract

In a large bowl, stir together the flour, sugar, and salt. Using a pastry blender or clean hands, cut or press the butter into the flour mixture until the mixture has small chunks of butter running throughout. In a small bowl, stir together the egg, cold water, and vanilla. Pour the egg mixture into the flour mixture, and use a fork to stir it together until a shaggy dough forms. Turn the dough out onto a work surface. Gently knead the dough until it comes together in a large mass. It will still be a bit shaggy.

Lightly flour the work surface and place the dough on top. Using a rolling pin, roll out the dough into a rectangle 15 to 18 inches long. Fold the dough into thirds, turn it 90 degrees on the work surface, and repeat to roll and fold the dough two more times. By the time you reach the third fold, your dough should be much more cohesive. Wrap the dough tightly in plastic wrap and chill for at least 30 minutes before using.

To partially bake your crust: On a lightly floured work surface, using a rolling pin, roll the chilled dough into a large circle ⅛- to ¼-inch thick. This is a generous amount of dough, so it will be enough for an 8- or 9-inch pie, and most deep-dish pie plates. Transfer the dough to the desired pie pan and trim the edges, leaving about 1 inch of overhang. Tuck the dough overhang underneath itself on the rim of the pan. Crimp your crust to your liking. Place the dough-lined pan into the freezer for 20 to 30 minutes. Meanwhile, preheat your oven to 350°F. Remove the pie crust from the freezer, and line the crust securely with foil. Fill the crust with pie weights all the way to the top of the crust. Bake until the foil pulls away from the crust easily, 15 to 20 minutes. Proceed as directed in your recipe.

To fully bake your crust: Follow the same instructions as par-baking. After 15 to 20 minutes of baking, remove the foil and the pie weights, then return the crust to the oven until the crust is light golden brown, 12 to 15 minutes. Proceed as directed in your recipe.

SAVORY PIE CRUST

This crust is a cross between a flaky pie dough and a crisp, cheesy cracker. It's salty, flaky, and perfect for nonsweet pies and quiches. You can make this crust in a food processor (use quick pulses and try not to process the mixture too much), but it will be much flakier if you make the dough by hand. This is perfect for the Broccoli Gruyère Quiche (page 208).

MAKES ONE 8- TO 9-INCH CRUST

1 cup all-purpose flour

½ teaspoon freshly ground black pepper

½ teaspoon onion powder

½ teaspoon dried oregano

¼ cup cold butter

1½ cups shredded cheddar cheese (from a block, not pre-shredded)

2 to 3 tablespoons milk

In a large bowl, stir together the flour, black pepper, onion powder, and oregano. Using a pastry blender or clean hands, cut or press the cold butter into the flour mixture until there are small, pea-sized chunks of butter running throughout the mixture. Toss the cheese through the mixture to coat it evenly in flour. Using a fork, stir in 2 tablespoons of milk, adding more if needed, until the dough can be easily pressed together with your fingers and holds shape. Now the dough is ready to roll, chill, and bake according to your recipe.

CHEESE CRACKER CRUST

You've heard of graham cracker crusts, but this savory version uses cheese crackers to create a salty, cheesy crust that's perfect for any quiche recipe. It's super easy to make and uses just two ingredients. If you don't have a food processor, just put the crackers in a plastic bag and crush them up with a rolling pin. Try this for the Ham & Cheddar Quiche (page 200).

MAKES ONE 8- TO 9-INCH CRUST

2 cups cheese crackers

¼ cup butter, melted

Preheat your oven to 350°F. In a food processor, grind the cheese crackers to a fine powder. Transfer the cheese crumbs to a bowl and stir in the melted butter until well incorporated. Press the mixture into an 8- to 9-inch pie pan. Bake the crust until lightly golden and firm to the touch, about 5 minutes to set it. Proceed as directed in your recipe.

SIMPLE PIZZA DOUGH

I love this recipe for a breakfast pizza, but it's also the perfect dough for any pizza that you like. If you really want to develop the flavor, make the dough a few days ahead of time and let it sit in the fridge to lightly ferment. It'll be chewier and more flavorful, but it's wonderful even without the extra chilling time. This is easiest to do in a stand mixer. Try it in the Breakfast Pizza on page 203.

MAKES DOUGH FOR 1 LARGE PIZZA

1¼ cup warm water (110°F to 115°F)

2 tablespoons olive oil

2¼ teaspoons active dry yeast

1 teaspoon sugar

2½ to 3 cups all-purpose flour

1 teaspoon salt

In the bowl of a stand mixer fitted with the dough hook attachment or in a large bowl, stir together the warm water, olive oil, yeast, and sugar. Let the mixture stand until foamy and bubbly, 5 to 10 minutes.

Add 2½ cups of flour and the salt to the mixer bowl. Mix on medium speed until the dough is smooth, sticky, soft, and elastic, about 10 minutes. The dough should be balling up around the dough hook but sticking to the bottom of the bowl. If the dough is sticking to the sides and pooling at the bottom, add more flour until it pulls away from the sides. Place the dough into an oiled bowl and cover with plastic wrap. Let the dough rest in the fridge for at least 2 hours, and up to 4 days before using.

LIME CURD

I love spreading citrus curd on top of toast or pancakes in the morning, and it's such an easy way to brighten up any breakfast dish. This recipe uses fresh limes, but you can make this with any citrus you like; I prefer the tart citrus options like lime, lemon, and grapefruit.

MAKES 1½ CUPS

3 eggs

2 to 3 tablespoons finely grated lime zest (from about 4 large limes)

⅔ cup lime juice (from about 4 large limes)

¾ cup sugar

⅛ teaspoon salt

2 tablespoons butter

In a saucepan, whisk together the eggs, lime zest, lime juice, sugar, and salt. Cook the mixture over medium heat, whisking constantly, until it becomes thick. This should take 8 to 10 minutes.

Remove the pan from the heat and whisk in the butter while it's still hot. Then, push the mixture through a fine mesh sieve into a bowl to remove any lumps or cooked egg bits. Place a sheet of plastic wrap directly on top of the curd, and chill the mixture for at least 2 hours, then enjoy on toast or pancakes!

CINNAMON-SUGAR COATING

1 cup granulated sugar

2 teaspoons ground cinnamon

For the cinnamon-sugar coating, in a bowl with room for tossing the sugar around, stir together the sugar and cinnamon.

CHOCOLATE ICING

2 cups powdered sugar

2 tablespoons Dutch process cocoa powder

2 to 4 tablespoons water

⅛ teaspoon salt

To make the chocolate icing, in a bowl, whisk together the powdered sugar, cocoa powder, 2 tablespoons water, and the salt. Add more water if needed to reach a consistency that drips off your whisk in a thick ribbon.

HIGH-ALTITUDE CONVERSION CHART

Over the years, I've received dozens of requests for an easy tool to help my followers convert standard baking recipes to work in their high-altitude kitchen. The following tricks have helped me. Use these as a starting point and make adjustments as needed for your own specific environment.

		ADJUSTMENT
CAKES	Flour	Increase by ¼ to ½ cup
	Sugar	Decrease by 1 teaspoon per cup
	Leavener	Decrease by 25%
	Liquid	Increase by 1 to 2 tablespoons
YEASTED BREADS	Rise Time	Decrease your rise time and check visual cues instead
	Kneading Time	Increase your kneading time by 5 to 8 minutes
QUICK BREADS, SCONES, MUFFINS	Flour	Increase by 2 to 4 tablespoons
	Leavener	Decrease by 25%
	Liquid	Increase by 2 to 3 teaspoons
	Rest time	Rest batters and doughs for 30 to 45 minutes
PANCAKES & WAFFLES	Flour	Increase by 2 to 4 tablespoons
	Leavener	Decrease by 25%
	Rest time	Rest batters and doughs for 30 to 45 minutes
SAVORY COOKING	Liquid	Increase by 2 to 4 tablespoons
	Cook time	Increase by 1 to 5 minutes

INDEX

Note: Page references in *italic* indicate photographs.

ABOUT THE AUTHOR

Nicole Hampton is the author of *Sugar High* and the writer behind DoughEyed.com, where she shares sweet and savory high-altitude-friendly recipes. Nicole has been featured in *5280 Magazine*, *The Washington Post*, *Colorado Life*, and *Colorado Country Life*.

Nicole lives in Denver, Colorado, at 5,000 feet above sea level. When she's not baking, you can find her working in digital marketing, reading, listening to podcasts, and eating breakfast for every single meal.

ACKNOWLEDGMENTS

This book has been a big hurdle for me as a writer and recipe developer, and I couldn't have done it without the unending support of those around me.

Mom and Dad, thank you for instilling in me a love of baking at such a young age, for cooking meals for me every single day (which feels completely insane to me now), and for literally making breakfast every single weekend. It's what I miss most about living with you!

To Jesse, thank you for always being there to make me a better photographer, to help when I break my camera, and for knowing more about it all than I probably ever will. Your encouragement for me as a food photographer has given me more confidence in something that I never thought I was good at.

To the many people I call family, thank you for eating it all, giving me recipe ideas, and supporting me at every event for the last few years. Katelyn, Spencer, Kari, Gabby, Kris, Lenny, Alec, Hannah, Matt, Courtney—I don't know how I'd do any of it without you in my life.

Everyone who helped me test recipes, we really made this book together. I'm so lucky to know people who love being in the kitchen as much as I do, and I can only aspire to one day be the wonderful cooks and bakers that you all are!

To Jen, Angie, Rachel, Olivia, and everyone at West Margin Press, thank you for your feedback, and your drive to make this the best book we could. I can't believe we've written another book together, and I'm so very grateful to have a team like you working so hard on this alongside me. Without you, I wouldn't be an author, and sometimes I still can't believe that I am one!

To Jacob, for all the dishes washed, breakfasts eaten, grocery store trips, and so much more, this whole book is for you. Thank you once again for all your support while I took huge amounts of time in our life and dedicated it to writing another book, this time with a child in the house no less! Your willingness to help me think of recipes, and to honestly critique them, has made me a better baker over the years. Here's to a lifetime of sharing breakfast any time of day with you.

Finally, to all the readers of this book, of *Sugar High*, and the readers at Dough-Eyed. It's been a wild couple of years for me with so many home bakers finding my book and finding me online. I feel nothing less than the luckiest person alive for being let into your kitchens every day and baking alongside you.

Text and Photographs © 2021 by Nicole Hampton

Library of Congress Cataloging-in-Publication Data

Names: Hampton, Nicole, author.
Title: High-altitude breakfast : sweet & savory baking at 5000 feet and
    above / Nicole Hampton.
Description: Berkeley : West Margin Press, 2021. | Includes index. |
    Summary: "Accompanied with beautiful photographs, this cookbook
    features specially created breakfast recipes when cooking or baking
    at high altitudes of 5000 feet and above"-- Provided by publisher.
Identifiers: LCCN 2021021084 (print) | LCCN 2021021085 (ebook) |
    ISBN 9781513289540 (paperback) | ISBN 9781513289571 (hardback)
    | ISBN 9781513289588 (ebook)
Subjects: LCSH: Breakfasts. | Baking. | High altitude cooking. |
    LCGFT: Cookbooks.
Classification: LCC TX733 .H348 2021 (print) | LCC TX733 (ebook) |
    DDC 641.5/2--dc23
LC record available at https://lccn.loc.gov/2021021084
LC ebook record available at https://lccn.loc.gov/2021021085

Edited by Jennifer Newens and Jessica Gould
Indexed by Elizabeth Parson
Image credit: page 232 Juan Sipion, J Gray Media

Proudly distributed by Ingram Publisher Services

LS2021

Published by West Margin Press®

WEST
MARGIN
PRESS

WestMarginPress.com

WEST MARGIN PRESS
Publishing Director: Jennifer Newens
Marketing Manager: Alice Wertheimer
Project Specialist: Micaela Clark
Editor: Olivia Ngai
Design & Production: Rachel Lopez Metzger